SETTING THE RECORD STRAIGHT
MORMONS
POLYGAMY

Cover: The symbols on the front cover are universally recognized as one male and two female figures. Of the twenty percent of Mormon families who practiced polygamy in the nineteenth-century, most had one husband and two wives.

SETTING THE RECORD STRAIGHT

MORMONS & POLYGAMY

Jessie L. Embry

Millennial Press, Inc.
P.O. Box 1741
Orem, UT 84059

ISBN: 1-932597-40-9

Cover design and typesetting by Adam Riggs

Dedication

To the interviewees who shared their stories in the LDS Polygamy and LDS Family Life Oral History Projects, Charles Redd Center for Western Studies, Brigham Young University.

Contents

Preface

Few members of The Church of Jesus Christ of Latter-day Saints understand why nineteenth-century Mormons practiced polygamy. Those outside of the Church are equally unsure. While I do not want to be known as the polygamy scholar, I am pleased to offer this short volume that answers some of the questions that many Mormons and non-Mormons ask about the subject.

Many people have helped with my research and writing of this study. I have learned so much from the scholars who wrote about polygamy before my 1987 book and those who have published since then. I am amazed by their careful examination of the sources and their abilities to tease out information where I did not think it existed.

I appreciate the help of Randy Bott from Millennial Press for providing the questions that BYU students ask him. Lindsey Shumway, the Marketing Director at Millennial Press, has been a joy to work with. I also am so very grateful for the docents at the Museum of Church History and Art—especially my Saturday friends—for reading an early version of the manuscript and asking additional questions. These include William T. Bingham, Isabel Erickson, Dorthene Richardson, Betty Ulmer, Ann Olmsted Holmes, Ann Benson, Connie Bauer, and Ann Kartchner-Hauley.

Claudia Shelton and Ann Olmsted Holmes went beyond

my initial request for questions and read the manuscript again. Ann describes herself as "a picky, picky copy editor at heart." I am grateful for her pickiness. It makes me look better.

Chronology

1830s

Joseph Smith, Jr. received a revelation to practice polygamy and married his first wife (wives).

1843

Smith recorded the revelation in hopes that his wife Emma Hales Smith would accept the principle. She did not.

1846

Mormon leaders acknowledged to other church members at Winter Quarters that they had plural wives.

1847

The first group of Mormons arrived in the Great Salt Lake Valley.

1852

Church President Brigham Young asked Apostle Orson Pratt to publicly announce that The Church of Jesus Christ of Latter-day Saints practiced polygamy.

1856

The Republican Party's platform included a statement against the "twin relics of barbarism slavery and polygamy."

1862

The United States Congress passed the Morrill Act, the first legislation against the Mormon practice of polygamy.

1870

The U.S. Congress does not pass the Cullom Bill which would had strengthened the Morrill Act.

The Utah Territorial Legislature gave women the right to vote.

1874

The U.S. Congress passed the Poland Act to strengthen the Morrill law.

1879

The U.S. Supreme Court heard George Reynolds case and decided in Reynolds v. U.S. that polygamy did not follow under freedom of religion.

1880s

Mormon polygamists went into hiding or moved to escape federal marshals. Some were sent to prison.

1882

The U.S. Congress passed the Edmunds Act which made polygamy a felony and cohabitation a misdemeanor.

1885

Some Mormons moved to Mexico to escape federal marshals. They were allowed to bring their plural wives.

1886

Some Mormons moved to Canada to escape federal marshals. They were not allowed to bring their plural wives.

1887

The U.S. Congress passed the Edmunds-Tucker Act which strengthened the Edmunds Act, took away Utah women's right to vote, and put church property in receivership.

1890

The U.S. Congress considered the Struble-Cullom Bill which would have increased penalties against polygamy.

Church President Wilford Woodruff issued a press release which said the Mormon Church had not performed marriages "contrary to the laws of the land."

1899

The U.S. Congress refused to seat Brigham H. Roberts, a Mormon General Authority and a polygamist, in the House of Representatives.

1904

Church President Joseph F. Smith issued the Second Manifesto which explained that those who continued to marry or perform plural marriages would be excommunicated.

1907

After a four-year debate, the U.S. Congress agreed to seat Reed Smoot, a Mormon Apostle and a monogamist, in the Senate.

1911

Matthias Cowley and John W. Taylor., Mormon Apostles were disciplined for performing marriages after 1904.

1918

Church President Heber J. Grant and Counselor J. Rueben Clark excommunicated those who continued to practice polygamy.

1935

The Utah State Legislature made unlawful cohabitation a felony.

1940s and 1950s

Utah and Arizona police raid Short Creek (now Colorado City), Arizona and arrest those who continued to practice polygamy.

1985

U.S. Supreme Court refused to hear Royston Potter's case against his firing as a Murray City, Utah police (Potter v. Murray City) and upheld Reynolds v U.S.

Why Study Mormon Polygamy?

Almost everyone who has heard of The Church of Jesus Christ of Latter-day Saints (also called Mormons, Latter-day Saints, or LDS) has heard about the Church's historical practice of men marrying more than one wife. Many believe that Latter-day Saints continue to have multiple marriages even though Church leaders abolished the practice more than a century ago. This book discusses Mormon polygamy and answers some of the more commonly asked questions.

Why has the Mormon Church been known for the practice of polygamy? Joseph Smith Jr., the Church's founder, introduced the concept during the Victorian period. Men and women had definite roles: men were the providers, and women were the nurturers. Americans were shocked when groups like the Mormons, the Shakers, and the Oneida Community changed those patterns with unique marriage practices—polygamy among the Mormons, celibacy among the Shakers, and "free love" among the Oneidians.

In addition, Mormons had a closed community. They worshipped together, they shared economic resources, and they voted as a bloc. Governmental officials disliked the power of the Church's leaders. Mormons saw Smith and his successors—Brigham Young, John Taylor, and Wilford Woodruff—as prophets and followed their counsel in all aspects of life. This concerned politicians, but they were not convinced that the av-

Brigham Young

erage voter cared about political issues. They knew that unusual marriage practices would shock Christian groups into action.

Finally, some people have an unusual desire to hear sensual stories about sex and violence. The forbidden often attracts attention. Many Americans felt that they were restricted by society's norms. They enjoyed reading about people who broke them. At the same time, they felt that those who set new rules should be forced to comply with societal norms. This continues today. Television shows on crime and unusual marriage patterns are popular for similar reasons. In 2007 these included *CSI, Sex in the City,* and *Desperate Housewives.*

Mormon polygamy filled the need for tales of sex in the nineteenth century. Even today the press continues to do stories about individuals who practice polygamy. These individuals, however, are not members of The Church of Jesus Christ of Latter-day Saints. For example, Warren Jeffs, leader of the Fundamentalist Church of Jesus Christ of Latter Day Saints, was never a member of the LDS Church. He ended up on the FBI's list of Ten Most-Wanted Fugitives, charged with forcing an underaged girl to marry an older man.

While many know that at one time members of The Church of Jesus Christ of Latter-day Saints practiced polygamy, LDS members and nonmembers alike often have misconceptions. When did the practice start? How long did the Church sanction such marriages? Who married plural wives? What percentage of Mormon families was polygamous? How were plural families organized? The following narrative history examines these questions.

As a single female historian and member of The Church of Jesus Christ of Latter-day Saints, I have seen people become alarmed when I tell them that the Mormon Church's historical practice of polygamy does not bother me. But polygamy for me is a historical fact that I study. I do not think about its possible impact on me. The LDS Church is as much against polygamy now as it was for it in the nineteenth century. I know that I will not be asked to marry a man who already has a wife. I have no idea what will happen in the next life, and I do not worry about polygamy then. Yet I do feel it is essential that both members and nonmembers learn about the history of Mormon polygamy before drawing any conclusions about Joseph Smith and why he and his followers accepted such an unusual practice.

Mormon Polygamy in a Nutshell

Some background will help readers understand my views. It is not clear when Joseph Smith received the revelation on plural marriage, but it was probably in the early 1830s. It is also unknown when he married his first plural wife. He recorded the revelation on plural marriage in 1843 to address the concerns of his first wife, Emma. Church leaders didn't publicly announce their practice of plural marriage until 1852. Four years later, in 1856, the Republican Party voiced opposition to the practice. Congress passed the first law outlawing polygamy in U.S. territories in 1862. From then until 1890, when Church president Wilford Woodruff issued the Manifesto ending plural marriage, Congress and the Mormons battled over polygamy.

In 1904 Church president Joseph F. Smith issued what historians call the Second Manifesto. After that edict was issued, those who continued to marry plural wives or perform plural marriages were excommunicated. Some present-day polygamists may trace their beginnings to Joseph Smith, but the LDS Church does not accept them as members.

Polygamy was practiced for a short period of time without any real opposition. In total, Mormons practiced polygamy for a little more than two generations. Some children grew up in polygamous homes and then started their own, but the practice did not continue to a third generation. Therefore, unlike other societies that have allowed plural marriages for generations, Mormons did not have time to establish rules on how husbands, wives, and children should relate to each other before. For example, following her study of plural families in Kenya, anthropologist Beatrice B. Whiting wrote, "Each wife had her own house and hearth and cared for her home, children, and animals."[1]

I argue in this book and in my previous study, *Mormon Polygamous Families: Life in the Principle,* that the Mormons adopted monogamous traditions in establishing their polygamous families. Husbands related to most of their wives in traditional ways. How families divided their time, how the wives interacted, and how the children reacted to having other "mothers" followed patterns that were similar to what their parents had grown up with. Wives of the same husband shared relationships similar to sisters. Children saw their father's other wives as aunts. The relationship for which there was no previous pattern was husband to multiple wives, so the men and women worked out a schedule in which each wife had her own time with her husband.

Why Study Mormon Polygamy

In May 2007 the Public Broadcasting System (PBS) aired a four-hour special titled *The Mormons.* Nationally known documentary producer Helen Whitney spent four years researching the LDS Church's history and members in the twentieth-first century. She interviewed more then eight hundred people about the past and present. The program's first two hours focused on Mormon history; its final two hours dealt with present-day Latter-day Saints. Whitney studied the Mormons because most Americans know little about the LDS Church, even though it was founded in the United States. Those who do know about the Church fear the control its leaders have over its members. That is one reason, according to a February 2007 Gallup Poll, that 72 percent of respondents reported that they would not vote for a Mormon as president of the United States.[2]

Journalists asked Whitney about Mormonism's greatest challenge. She responded that Mormons have a "messy history and theology" that is not easy to explain. Nevertheless, she encouraged Latter-day Saints to "own" their past and beliefs. Part of that "messy history," she said, is the Mormon Church's practice of polygamy. Why? Because when pollsters asked Americans what they knew about Mormons, the most frequent response was polygamy.[3]

The University of Utah's KUED and Brigham Young University's KBYU (both PBS stations) sponsored a *Utah Now* program about Whitney's show. KUED documentary producer Ken Verdoia explained that the popular view of Mormons is of old men with beards and many wives. He said the documentary would have a true impact if it changed that popular image. Verdoia wondered, however, if there would be a change because Whitney's documentary spent almost half an hour discussing Mormon polygamy.

Whitney gave three reasons for focusing so much time on polygamy. First, she said that plural marriage was the reason that the Mormon Church experienced so many problems during the nineteenth century. Rumors of polygamy, along with closed economic and political communities, forced the Mormons to move and rebuild their lives outside the United States. Second, the Mormons practiced polygamy because they believed it was ordained of God. This shows, she said, the extent to which Mormons will go to obey what they feel is God's will.

The third reason Whitney identified was that the Mormons' practice of polygamy affected American constitutional history. Mormons appealed to the Supreme Court, claiming that their practice of polygamy was protected under freedom of religion. The court declared in *Reynolds v. the United States* that the U.S. Constitution protected belief but not practices. This case still determines how courts look at religious beliefs and practices.

The Mormon Church and the Study of Polygamy

Despite these compelling reasons to study polygamy, the Mormon Church commented little about plural marriage in its publications during the twentieth century and continues that practice in the twentieth-first century. In the 1990s the Church started a new curriculum in its weekly priesthood meetings for men and in its weekly Relief Society meetings for women. The Church's curriculum committee selects themes that are important to past presidents, basing the lessons on their teachings. Brigham Young was the first president to be studied. Some LDS historians were upset that in an entire manual on one of the most married men in Mormon history, the topic of polygamy was never mentioned.

The reaction of these historians is surprising. The Mormon Church seldom mentions polygamy in its publications. Church magazines carry historical articles but rarely mention polygamy.

That pattern continues in other areas of church communication. The Church of Jesus Christ of Latter-day Saints' official web page (ldschurch.org) includes a history of each president of the Church with a timeline of birth, dates as president, and other important events. Marriage is not listed for any presidents until George Albert Smith, who became the Church's president in 1945. Why? My guess is that Joseph Smith, Brigham Young, John Taylor, Wilford Woodruff, Lorenzo Snow, Joseph F. Smith, and Heber J. Grant—the presidents who preceded George Albert Smith—had multiple wives. For Joseph Smith and Brigham Young, it is difficult to even determine how many wives they had. For the rest it would be a list that the Church does not want to focus on.

This pattern did upset me at one time. But it no longer bothers me. Do I believe that the Church is trying to hide its history? Maybe a little. No one wants to be remembered for something that can be as misunderstood as plural marriage. But I believe there is a more important reason. There are groups that continue to practice polygamy. Some trace their beginnings to Joseph Smith and John Taylor. The Church does not want to appear to support these groups in any way. Church leaders expect that these groups would use any positive statement about plural marriage by LDS leaders to support their claims that Church leaders are in apostasy. Equally important, leaders work hard to present the Church as a mainline Christian church and its members as all-American. Polygamy does not fit in that image.

The programs *The Mormons* and *Utah Now* reinforced my views about why the Church does not discuss polygamy. After discussing the history of Mormon polygamy, Whitney ended part one of her program with the story of a modern-day polygamous family. While representatives of the Mormon Church carefully pointed out that the Church has not practiced polygamy for a century, a family of practicing polygamists—a handsome husband, three beautiful wives, and several cute children—was the last picture viewers saw the first night. With that image in mind, what is the answer to Ken Verdoia's question of what will be the impact of the documentary? It might be that Mormons are still polygamists although the beards are gone.

It's easy to see why the Church seldom discusses polygamy. It does not want to provide support for groups that continue the practice, and it does not want to be associated with those groups. Members are specifically asked not to associate with groups that support practices that are opposed to current church teachings, and they can be denied temple recommends if they do. Church leaders know that when many people hear of Mormons, they immediately think of polygamy. Discussion of the topic does not remove that image; it may even enhance the belief that Mormon men still have multiple wives.

Personal Experience

Does that mean that LDS Church leaders prevent the study of plural marriage? No. As a researcher, I looked at the Church's past and still remained in the Church—and even in church employment.

In 1976 I was an oral history interviewer for the Charles Redd Center for Western Studies at the LDS Church-owned Brigham Young University. That year Maude T. Bentley, the third wife of Joseph C. Bentley, a church leader in the Mormon Colonies in Mexico, passed away. She had been a widow for many years, so she had not been living polygamy. But she had been a plural wife. Eugene Campbell, a BYU professor, an important Utah historian, and a member of the Redd Center board, suggested that the Oral History Program at the Charles Redd Center had missed a chance to interview a participant in a unique aspect of Mormon history. Campbell added that the children of Church-sanctioned plural marriages were then in their seventies and eighties, and unless some efforts were made to collect their stories, they would be lost.

The Redd Center's director, Thomas G. Alexander, and the Oral History Program director, John V. Bluth, agreed. They assigned me to interview children who grew up in families of Church-sanctioned plural marriages. Because the center started the program in the 1970s, few of the children were still alive, and they represented the end of Mormon polygamy. But I was able to contact and interview a number of people. Not everyone I found agreed to be interviewed. I believe that some refused because of unhappy family situations. But most who refused did not want to share their stories because of a request by Church leaders to polygamous husbands and wives at the end of plural marriage not to discuss the subject. Those who agreed to be interviewed talked to me because I worked for BYU, and I was a recently returned missionary. I was not from a group that continued the practice of plural marriage.

I did interviews for about six months, and then funds for my temporary employment ended. I went on to another temporary job for the LDS Church's Historical Department and was assigned to document the experiences of Mormon women. This included Camilla Eyring Kimball, the wife of Spencer W. Kimball, then Church president. Sister Kimball's father, Edward Christian Eyring, had two wives. As an interviewer for the Redd Center, I had talked to some of her full brothers and sisters. Later, Redd Center employees talked to her half brothers and sisters. I was uneasy on how to approach the subject with the Church president's wife, but she made it easy for me. Before I started the interview, she said, "I am a child of a polygamous family. Let's not leave that out."

In 1979 I became the Oral History Program director at the Charles Redd Center. During my absence from the center, the center continued to interview children of polygamous families. It was my main project as well. By the time the project was completed, the center had collected 250 interviews. As I listened to the interviews, I decided that there was no set pattern for Mormon polygamous families, so I started another set of interviews to look at Mormon monogamous families. The Redd Center conducted 150 interviews for that project. The interviews became a control group to compare Mormon polygamous families with monogamous families.

I believed that the best way to let scholars know about these oral history interviews was to write a book based on them. Redd Center Director Thomas G. Alexander agreed. To help me get started, I decided to offer a class on Mormon family life at BYU. The Honors Program agreed to list the class, and I started publicity. The college newspaper, *The Daily Universe,* sent a reporter to ask me about the class. Because I knew that the Church rarely discussed polygamy, I gave guarded answers and stressed that I would discuss Mormon family life in the nineteenth century. The newspaper's editor was not happy with the article and sent the reporter back to question me about polygamy. I answered the questions, and the reporter discussed polygamy in the article.

The article raised questions for the university administration. Through the chain of authority, I received word that the president of the university was concerned. He said he had not approved the class and wanted to see the course outline. I had not created one yet because I was not sure that anyone would sign up for the class. But in response to his request, I created a course outline that was approved. However, no one signed up for the class. I figured that was because it was not a required class and did not meet any general education requirement. But my time was not wasted; the outline became the basis for my 1987 book.

At the time I believed that I was writing the definitive study of Mormon polygamy. Of course, I was wrong. As I have matured as a historian, I recognize that will never happen. There will always be something new to say on the subject. I have not wanted to be known as the person who does polygamy, so I moved on to other subjects. Interestingly enough, my next oral history project was on African-American Mormons, another difficult subject because of the restriction on blacks holding the priesthood in the Church before 1978. My research on these two highly debated topics—blacks and the priesthood and polygamy—has not affected my employment at BYU.

After my book was published, the LDS Church public relations department asked me to research and write an article in response to claims that Mormons practiced incest. Church employees were responding to concerns by members of the Church that books on child abuse quoted a 1915 article by Theodore Schroeder titled "Incest in Mormonism." It seemed that scholars doing a literature search on incest found Schroeder's article in the *American Journal of Urology and Sexology*. As I will discuss later, the problem was a definition of terms. Mormon men often married sisters, and Schroeder considered this incest. I looked carefully at all of Schroeder's examples and then wrote an article that was published in the *Journal of Mormon History*.[4] The hope was that those searching the subjects of Mormonism and incest would find my article in addition to Schroeder's.

I was willing to research the topic suggested by the LDS Church, which owns my employer, BYU. However, I was not willing to discuss the virtues of polygamy when private-sector attorneys asked me to testify in a modern-day polygamy case. In this instance, a woman with children married a man who already had wives. When the woman died, her sisters wanted to remove the children from the polygamous family because, they argued, polygamy was not a safe environment. The attorneys wanted me to say, based on my historical research, that children in polygamous families grew up with support and love.

I believed that my employer would not approve of me making the connection between historical, Mormon-sanctioned plural marriages and those who practice polygamy contrary to the teachings of the Church since 1904. When I discuss plural marriage, I always carefully point out that I am talking about a historical event that is in the past.

That does not mean that there has not been some concern by BYU administrators about the study of polygamy. D. Michael Quinn, a former BYU professor, was one of several scholars excommunicated by the Church in 1995. Quinn wrote a lengthy article that was published in *Dialogue: A Journal of Mormon Thought*. He listed all the marriages performed after 1890, when Wilford Woodruff issued the Manifesto ending marriages contrary to the laws of the land. Quinn's thesis was that the Manifesto was only a political move and that LDS Church leaders continued to sanction such marriages.[5]

Studies on Mormon Polygamy

My study and Quinn's study are not unique. Polygamy is one of the most studied aspects of Mormon history. Latter-day Saints and non-Latter-day Saints alike have examined the practice from many angles. In 1954 Kimball Young, a sociologist, published *Isn't One Wife Enough?* Young, a descendant of Brigham Young and Heber C. Kimball, Mormon leaders who had many wives, was not a practicing Mor-

Stanley Ivins

mon. Despite the title his publisher gave the book, the author concluded that most plural families were successful.

Stanley S. Ivins, son of Anthony W. Ivins, who performed plural marriages in Mexico, wrote an article published in the *Utah Historical Quarterly* in 1967 that was the main source of information on the subject for years.

B. Carmon Hardy, who taught history at California State University-Fullerton, wrote a dissertation on polygamy in Mexico in 1963 and has published several books and documentary studies on Mormon plural marriage. His work focused on the time period between 1890 and 1904 and discussed the religious motivations for polygamy and its place in Mormon doctrine.

In 1986 Richard Van Wagoner wrote a general survey titled *Mormon Polygamy: A History,* which gives a summary of the practice. His book came out at the same time as my study, *Mormon Polygamous Families: Life in the Principle,* which was based on interviews conducted by Kimball Young and his research assistant, James Hulett, and on oral histories recorded by the Charles Redd Center.

Several studies have focused on the practice of polygamy in selected Mormon communities. Humboldt State professor and geographer Lowell "Ben" Bennion looked at polygamy in Washington County, in southern Utah; and in Davis County, just north of Salt Lake County. BYU professor Kathryn M. Daynes examined plural marriage in Manti, Sanpete County, in central Utah.

Bennion and Daynes, along with University of Utah architectural historian Thomas Carter, are looking at several communities in Utah where plural families lived. They're also looking for better answers to questions such as how many Mormon families were polygamists and how many plural marriages ended in divorce.

Sarah Gordon, a historian and law professor at the University of Pennsylvania, looked at the writings and legal aspects of nineteenth-century Mormon polygamy. Other scholars have examined modern-day polygamists, who LDS Church members and leaders believe have left the fold. Former BYU professor Martha Sonntag Bradley, now a professor at the University of Utah, wrote about the raids at Short Creek, Arizona, headquarters of the Fundamentalist Church of Jesus Christ of Latter Day Saints, in the 1950s. Utah and Arizona authorities had attempted to eliminate polygamy by putting men in jail and women and children in foster care. The attempt failed. When the men were released from jail, they returned to their families.

Ken Driggs, an attorney, has studied those who continue to practice polygamy. Driggs does an excellent job of explaining the complex web of current polygamists, sometimes referred to as Mormon Fundamentalists. While Mormon leaders and members disagree with that term, many current polygamists see themselves as connected to the Mormon Church. Driggs's writings explain why, and they discuss disputes in modern-day polygamous communities. [6]

The studies mentioned so far deal strictly with polygamy. There are too many books and articles that mention plural marriage to list. General histories of the LDS Church by both Latter-day Saints and non-Latter-day Saints discuss plural marriage. Histories of selected time periods and communities show how polygamy affected Mormons.

One of the most interesting studies was Robert Bruce Flanders's *Nauvoo: Kingdom on the Mississippi,* published in 1965. At the time he wrote the book, Flanders was a professor at Graceland College, which was owned by the Reorganized Church of Jesus Christ of Latter Day Saints, known since 2001 as the Community of Christ. In his book, he discussed Joseph Smith's practice of plural marriage, something that the RLDS Church always denied.[7]

Biographies of Mormon Church leaders such as Joseph Smith and Brigham Young have sections on family life. The subject is also an important topic in histories of Emma Smith and her son Joseph Smith III. Latter-day Saints are encouraged to write family histories. Whether the books are published by academic presses, popular presses, or the authors, polygamy is nearly always mentioned if the ancestors lived the principle. While Latter-day Saint authors clearly point out that the Church does not continue the practice, they are proud of their ancestors who met the challenge. Jonathan Cannon, who grew up in a polygamous family, explained in an oral history interview, "It is strange that I would feel as monogamous as I feel and yet feel all the love and affection and appreciation of my parents who were polygamists."[8]

This book can only begin to explain the Mormon practice of polygamy. I answer some questions that both Latter-day Saints and those of other faiths frequently ask. Much has been written on the subject, and much can still be learned. To help the reader find out more information, the citations in this book refer to books and articles about Mormon polygamy. While I use quotes from journals, oral histories, and other primary sources, I cite the secondary sources. I have not included a note after each direct quote. Most of the references are from my book *Mormon Polygamous Families*. Interested readers can go to those books and articles to get the citations for the primary sources. My goal has been to cite books and articles that are readily available through libraries or interlibrary loan.

Notes

1.   Jessie L. Embry, *Mormon Polygamous Families: Life in*

the Principle (Salt Lake City: University of Utah Press, 1987), 74.

2.   Jeffrey M. Johnson, "Some Americans Reluctant to Vote for Mormon, 72-Year-Old Presidential Candidates," February 20, 2007," http://www. galluppoll.com/content/?ci=26611.

3.   Frank Newport, "Americans' Views of the Mormon Religion," March 2, 2007, http://www.galluppoll. com/content/?ci=26758&pg=1

4.   Jessie L. Embry, "Intimate Taboos: Incest and Mormon Polygamy," *Journal of Mormon History* 18 (1992): 93–113.

5.   D. Michael Quinn, "LDS Church Authority and New Plural Marriages, 1890–1904," *Dialogue: A Journal of Mormon Thought* 18 (Spring 1985): 9–105.

6.   Ken Driggs, "Twentieth-Century Polygamy and Fundamentalist Mormons in Southern Utah," *Dialogue: Journal of Mormon Thought* 24(Winter 1991):44-58.

7.   Robert Bruce Flanders, *Nauvoo: Kingdom on the Mississippi* (Urbana, Ill.: University of Illinois Press, 1965).

8.   Embry, *Mormon Polygamous Families*, xiii.

Beginnings
of Polygamy

Understanding the Church's beginnings helps understand why nineteenth century Mormons accepted plural marriage. In 1820 Joseph Smith Jr., a young farm boy living in New York state, wondered why there were so many religions and why their doctrines seemed so different. After reading James in the New Testament, he decided to follow James's counsel and pray. In response, he had a vision in which he saw God the Father and his son, Jesus Christ. They told him that the true church was not on the earth.

Three years later young Joseph received a vision from Moroni, an ancient prophet in the Americas who had buried some gold plates in a hillside about four hundred years after Christ. These plates were the history of a group of Israelites who left the Middle East in about 600 B.C. and traveled to the American continent under God's direction. Moroni told Smith that he would be asked to translate these plates.

Smith translated and published the record, now known as the Book of Mormon. Latter-day Saints declare that the book is another witness of Jesus Christ's divine mission because it tells of Christ's visit to the Americas after His resurrection. Some argue that Latter-day Saints are not Christians because they believe the Book of Mormon is scripture like the Bible. Non-Latter-day Saints are also concerned that Mormons believe that Jesus Christ and Heavenly Father are separate beings. Mormons insist that they worship the same God as other Christians. For them, the Book of Mormon, Doctrine and Covenants, and Pearl of Great Price, all seen as scriptures by Latter-day Saints, increase their understanding of God.

In 1830 God commanded Joseph Smith to organize a church, which started small with only six members, as required by law. Over the years missionaries traveled in the United States and Canada, then in England, and finally throughout the world. The Church grew from those six members to nearly thirteen million at the end of 2006. Church members declare that Smith was a prophet who proclaimed God's will to them and the rest of the world. He restored saving ordinances that allow people to return to the presence of God after this life. Latter-day Saints believe that Smith's successors are also prophets who have continued to give guidance and to explain God's will for men on earth. The Church of Jesus Christ of Latter-day Saints declares that God continues to guide people, who are literally His children.

Plan of Salvation

The belief that all those who live on earth are God's children is an important but unique part of LDS theology. According to LDS doctrine, all people lived as spirits in a pre-earth life. God, our Heavenly Father, created these spirits. But they were not equal to God because they did not have bodies like Him. To obtain bodies, these spirits needed to leave God's presence and be tested. The test required that the spirits not remember the previous life. Without that knowledge, they would still need to recognize God's commands.

When God presented this plan to the spirits, they rejoiced. But God recognized that everyone would not always follow His instructions. They would make mistakes, and if He were completely just, they could not return to His presence. He developed a plan that would allow for justice and mercy. Jesus Christ, God's oldest son, offered to provide the Atonement. Lucifer, a Son of the Morning, however, offered to force everyone to obey. God wanted the spirits to be able to choose on their own, so He accepted Christ's offer. Lucifer rebelled and caused a war in heaven. As a result, God cast Lucifer and his followers, a third of the spirits, out. Lucifer became Satan, or the devil, and his goal is to tempt God's children and lead them away from Heavenly Father's plan.

God, with the assistance of Jesus Christ and Michael (who became Adam, the first man on earth) created a world on which the spirits would dwell. Then God created Adam and Eve, as described in the Old Testament. Adam and Eve transgressed, were cut off from the direct presence of God, and became subject to death. Christ came in the meridian of time to provide the Atonement. He died on the cross, but because He was part God, the offspring of Heavenly Father and Mary, He had the power to be resurrected. His resurrection made it possible for all people to live again.

Christ promised that He would return at the end of the world. At that point there will be a judgment. This earth will become a celestial body for those who successfully passed their test on earth. The spirits of everyone who lived on earth will be united with their bodies. Those who followed God's plan will live in families on the perfected earth and will become gods. Lorenzo Snow, who became president of the Church, created a couplet that summarizes Smith's teachings and LDS doctrine:

"As man now is, God once was; as God is now man may be."[1]

Those who did not follow God's plan will still be resurrected but will live in other kingdoms described as terrestrial and telestial.

According to this plan, two major events must occur before Christ's second coming. First, everyone needs to have the opportunity to accept or reject God's plan. According to Joseph Smith, the plan, or gospel, was lost from the earth after Christ's death. God told Smith to restore the plan to the earth and to share this message with everyone on earth. Those who do not hear the message on earth will have a chance to do so in a pre-resurrected state after they die. Once they hear the message they can still accept or reject it. But they cannot be saved even if they accept it if they have not had saving ordinances (often referred to as sacraments in other religions). People on earth must perform these ordinances on earth. These sacraments for the dead take place in temples.

Church members do not know the wishes of those who have passed on, so they perform ordinances for as many people for whom they can find birth, death, and marriage information. However, baptism and other ordinances apply only if the unresurrected spirits accept the message. Otherwise, these ordinances are not binding.

One of the ordinances that occurs in the temple is marriage for life *and* eternity. The LDS phrase is marriage "for time and all eternity." Latter-day Saints believe that marriage does not have to end "until death do we part." If marriages are sealed by priesthood authority in the temple, Latter-day Saints believe, they can last forever. Children can also be sealed to their parents. Church members do family history work not only to make sure that their ancestors are baptized but also to create a family link throughout time.

The second major event that must occur before Christ's second coming is that all of God's spirit children need to receive a body. This requires that men and women marry and have children. Latter-day Saints believe that there are many spirits waiting to come to earth. If they restrict the number of their children, they are not fulfilling God's plan. Therefore, having children is a commandment.

Latter-day Saints believe that Joseph Smith restored this plan, playing an important role in the salvation of God's children. They also believe that Smith's successors have been prophets, seers, and revelators who speak for God. Church members believe that they should follow the counsel of these leaders. Sometimes they might not understand why, but they believe that obedience is essential. However, members believe that they do not have to follow blindly. Like their leaders, they can pray and learn whether the guidance is God's advice or the leaders' advice. They have been taught that God will not allow the Church's prophet to misinform the members or lead them astray. Therefore, God could command one prophet to obey a law such as polygamy. When situations changed, He could command a later prophet to discontinue the practice.

Understanding the Plan of Salvation

This plan of salvation or, as the Book of Mormon calls it, "the great plan of happiness" (Alma 42:8), is unique. Latter-day Saints want to share it with the world. For example, for the 1964 New York's World Fair, The Church of Jesus Christ of Latter-day Saints produced a film titled *Man's Search for Happiness* that describes this theology. After asking the questions "Who am I?" "Why am I here?" and "Where am I going after this life?" the film followed a family through the birth of a child to the death of a grandfather. The message Church leaders wanted to tell the world was that life is part of an eternal plan. Spirit children come to earth, where they receive a body and are tested.

Elder Merrill J. Bateman and his wife, Marilyn, expanded on this concept while Merrill was president of Brigham Young University. In an address to the BYU student body on January

14, 2003, they spelled out three purposes for coming to earth: to receive a body, to grow spiritually, and to have a family. Physical health is important to longevity on earth, they said, but our bodies will not always be the same. They will wear out. But there are no limits to spiritual growth. The Batemans added that creating eternal families is essential to further God's plan.[21]

Latter-day Saints believe that families are eternal. The relationship between a husband and a wife is sacred. Polygamy does not appear to fit into the picture. That is why 2008 presidential candidate Mitt Romney said in a *60 Minutes* interview that he felt polygamy was "awful."[3] It is as hard for present-day Latter-day Saints to understand as it is for nonmembers. It was equally as hard for early Mormons to accept. They only did so because of the counsel of Church leaders and a personal confirmation from God that it was right.

Historian Kathleen Flake tried to explain this concept in the documentary *The Mormons*. Referring to why the Mormons continued to practice polygamy even when plural marriage was against the law, she explained that it would be like the government telling people they could not baptize. But because most Christian religions consider baptism essential, she continued, they would find ways to baptize.

Latter-day Saints believe that God's ways are higher than man's ways and that there is not always a logical explanation for His instructions. Throughout the scriptures, there are times when the Lord asked His people to perform acts that they did not understand at the time. Abraham and Sarah prayed for a son. After Isaac's miraculous birth, the Lord commanded Abraham to sacrifice his son. Moses received the Ten Commandments, including the requirement "Thou shalt not kill" (Exodus 20: 13). Yet later the Lord required the children of Israel to kill all the Midianites. With hindsight, Abraham's willingness to sacrifice his son (even though he was saved at the last minute) becomes a symbol of God's sacrifice of his son Jesus so that all may be resurrected. God's instructions to Moses can be seen as a way to protect the children of Israel from worshipping the idols of the Midianites.[4]

Like these prophets, Joseph Smith heard the word of God and followed His counsel even if he did not understand it. His followers accepted Smith's word as God's will even if they could not understand it. The Church of Jesus Christ of Latter-day Saints is built on the belief that God speaks to humans, and following His commands is essential for happiness in this life and eternal life with God in the next existence.

Elder Richard G. Hinckley, a Mormon General Authority and the son of Church president Gordon B. Hinckley, explained the difficulty in understanding God's instructions. He pointed out that much of scientific knowledge is based on two theories—relativity and quantum mechanics. There are points where the two appear to contradict each other, but that does not mean that either is incorrect. Elder Hinckley continued with the example of a mason building a rock wall. If a rock does not fit, the mason does not throw it away. Rather, he sets it aside and waits until there is a place for it. Elder Hinckley then told his BYU audience that just like the mason, they do not always understand God's plan. But they need to live with the lack of knowledge just as scientists live with the differences between the theory of relativity and quantum mechanics.[5]

Many Latter-day Saints would like a better explanation for why God commanded early Church members to practice polygamy; unfortunately, there is not one. The only reason that makes any sense is that the early members followed God. Faith is difficult to explain. The Apostle Paul wrote in Hebrews 11:1 that faith is "the substance of things hoped for, the evidence of things not seen." Danish theologian Soren Kierkegaard described faith as a "leap." He explained that the leap is the most difficult step that dancers have because there is a time when they are in flight and do not know if they will land or fall. He concluded, "I can, I think, describe the movements of faith perfectly, but I can never perform them."[6]

Kierkegaard's words have been echoed by people who disbelieve because they cannot see and by religious leaders who use the concept as a way to support their beliefs. Elder Bruce R. McConkie of the Church's Quorum of the Twelve Apostles, wrote, "A special standard of judgment is needed to prove anything in the spiritual realm. No scientific research, no intellectual inquiry, no investigative processes known to mortal man can prove that God is a personal being, that all men will be raised in immortality, and that repentant souls are born of the Spirit. . . . Spiritual verities can be proven only by spiritual means."[7]

Elder Dallin H. Oaks, who trained as a lawyer and served on the Utah Supreme Court and as president of Brigham Young University before he became an Apostle, agreed. "What the scriptures call conversion—the change of mind and heart that gives us the direction and strength to move resolutely toward eternal life—comes only by the witness and power of the Holy Spirit."[8]

Polygamy, like all other aspects of Mormonism or other religious beliefs, requires communication with God. Like many other people, I struggle to know whether I am listening to God or listening to my own desires. But like other Latter-day Saints, I see that as part of life's test. Through reading the scriptures, praying, and mediating, I attempt to know God's will. I am often wrong and make mistakes. But that's why Jesus Christ accepted His mission. His atoning sacrifice makes it possible for me to change when I realize that I am not on the right course.

Beginnings of Mormon Polygamy[9]

Joseph Smith faced that same type of dilemma when he accepted God's request to marry more than one wife. Technically the Mormons practiced polygyny (a man married to more than one wife). Polygamy is the generic term meaning more than one spouse. Polyandry is a woman married to more than one man. However, Mormons did not make the distinction and referred to their practice as polygamy, plural marriage, or celestial marriage.

So how did polygamy begin in the LDS Church? In his attempt to learn God's will, Joseph Smith studied the Old Testament extensively. When he could not understand certain concepts, he prayed for guidance. In response, God answered and occasionally asked Smith to accept new doctrine. One question Smith asked God was why Old Testament leaders such as Abraham, Isaac, and Jacob had more than one wife. In response, the Lord told him, "Prepare thy heart to receive and obey the instructions which I am about to give unto you; for all those who have this law revealed unto them must obey the same" (D&C 132:3).

There are no clear records of when Smith received these instructions. He recorded the revelation, now section 132 in the Doctrine and Covenants, a book of his revelations, in 1843 in an attempt to convince his wife, Emma Hale Smith, that polygamy came from God. But the doctrine was not new. A few Church leaders knew of Smith's multiple marriages years before, and non-Mormons circulated rumors about the marriage practice at least ten years before.

How do historians know that section 132 was written years af-

Emma Smith

ter Joseph Smith started the practice? Verses 51 through 56 directly refer to Emma's opposition to polygamy. The revelation explained that she would be destroyed if she did not allow Joseph to marry additional wives. It is not clear when Emma first heard about polygamy, but she seemed to vary in her views. She was shocked when she learned that her friend Eliza R. Snow had married her husband. According to LDS sources, she later agreed and allowed Joseph to marry the Partridge sisters, Emma and Eliza (whom Joseph had already married in secret), and sisters Maria and Sarah Lawrence. Later she spoke against these marriages.

Joseph's brother Hyrum and other Church leaders suggested to Joseph that Emma might accept the revelation if she saw it in writing. She did not. Rumors are that after she saw the written revelation she burned it. Some sources suggest that if she did burn the revelation, it was with her husband's permission.

But Joseph Smith had discussed polygamy years before. On July 17, 1831, Church leader W. W. Phelps said Smith told him and others: "It is my will that in time, ye should take unto you wives of the Lamanites"—Indians, according to the Book of Mormon. Phelps questioned how he and others could take Indian wives given that the men were already married. Smith told him, "In the same manner that Abraham took Hagar and Keturah; and Jacob took Rachel, Bilhah and Zilpah, by Revelation." Some historians believe that Smith married his first plural wife, Fanny Alger, in 1835.

Smith told only selected leaders about plural marriage. Most of his followers did not know of the practice. But rumors spread quickly, and soon non-Mormons reacted to polygamy. Phelps, the editor of a Mormon newspaper and Smith's secretary, explained at a church meeting on August 17, 1835: "Inasmuch as this church of Christ has been reproached with the crime of fornication, and polygamy, we declare that we believe that one man should have one wife, and one woman but one husband, except in time of death."

Smith was in Michigan, and Church historian B. H. Roberts stated in the 1930s that Phelps introduced the topic without Smith's permission. Other studies suggest that Smith asked Phelps to make the statement to refute the rumors, even if they were correct.

The Mormons moved several times because of disagreement with their neighbors over economic, political, and religious philosophy. After moving from Kirtland, Ohio (near Cleveland), to Missouri (near Independence), the Mormons established a new home in Nauvoo, Illinois, on the Mississippi River, not far from St. Louis, Missouri. There, Smith told his closest associates about the revelation to marry plural wives. Brigham Young, who succeeded Smith as president and eventually married multiple times, recalled, "Some of the brethren know what my feelings were at the time Joseph revealed the doctrine; I was not desirous of shrinking from any duty, nor of failing in the lack to do as I was commanded, but it was the first time in my life that I desired the grave, and I could hardly get over it for a long time."

During the 1840s those like Young who knew of plural marriage used code words such as "celestial marriage" to hide the practice from the Church's enemies. However, some insiders left the Church partially because of polygamy. Two leaders, Wilson and William Law, published an anti-Mormon newspaper, the *Nauvoo Expositor.* Its primary theme was polygamy. Joseph Smith's decision to destroy the press led to his arrest and eventually his death.

Joseph Smith and Polygamy

Why did Joseph Smith accept a doctrine so foreign to his

upbringing? According to some accounts, an angel threatened Smith with a sword and told him that unless he obeyed the command to marry plural wives, he would lose his power as a prophet. Smith felt that he had no other choice. He taught his followers the same thing. Historian Richard L. Bushman wrote that Smith's comment to other Mormons was, "This is a revelation from God to your prophet. Seek your own inspiration and you will know for yourself. If you deny it, you will lose your blessings."[10]

According to historian Lawrence Foster, there are four ways to view Smith's practice of polygamy.[11]

1. Emma Smith taught her children that Joseph was never involved in polygamy. Brigham Young started polygamy. Because polygamy was practiced by only a few people in secret before the Mormons journeyed to Utah, it is difficult to find records about Joseph Smith's multiple wives.

2. Non-Mormons and anti-Mormons say that Joseph was oversexed and looking for a way to justify his passions. In 1945 Fawn McKay Brodie wrote in a psychological history of Joseph Smith: "Monogamy seemed to [Smith]—as it has seemed to many men who have not ceased to love their wives, but who have grown weary of connubial exclusiveness—an intolerably circumscribed way of life." Brodie quoted Smith as saying, "Whenever I see a pretty woman, I have to pray for grace." Brodie continued, "But Joseph was no careless libertine who could be content with clandestine mistresses. There was too much of the Puritan in him, and he could not rest until he had redefined the nature of sin and erected a stupendous theological edifice to support his new theories on marriage."[12]

3. Mormons believe Joseph Smith was doing the will of God. (This book presents that viewpoint.)

4. Historians and therapists have decided that Smith had psychological problems. Physician William D. Morain made

that argument in *The Sword of Laban: Joseph Smith, Jr. and the Dissociated Mind*, which was published by the American Psychiatric Press in 1998. In this book, Morain refers to an operation that Smith had as a child and then relates Book of Mormon stories and Smith's later life, including polygamy, to the stress Smith experienced then.[13]

Based on the records available, it is impossible to know which view is correct. But most histories agree that Smith married plural wives.

How many wives did Joseph Smith have? The numbers vary widely. Andrew Jensen, who worked as an assistant historian for the LDS Church, said Smith had twenty-seven. Brodie reported forty-eight. Historian D. Michael Quinn said thirty-six. Researcher George D. Smith came up with forty-three. Stanley S. Ivins said there were eighty-four.

One of the problems is defining *wife*. A number of women were sealed to Smith before and after his death. Until Church president Wilford Woodruff told Church members to research their own family lines, early members believed that they would receive greater blessings if they were sealed to a Church leader. Those women who wanted that blessing were not Smith's wives on earth. Author Todd Compton tried to give a complete count of Smith's wives on earth. Using as many sources as he could find, he identified thirty-three women in his biography of Smith's wives, *In Sacred Loneliness*. No evidence exists that Joseph Smith fathered children with any of his plural wives.[14]

Polygamy from 1844 to 1852

When Joseph Smith died in 1844, only twenty-nine men had married plural wives. The marriages were performed in secret. Once the Mormons left Nauvoo for Winter Quarters, Nebraska, Church members discussed plural marriage. Eliza R. Snow, who had married Joseph Smith in Nauvoo and then became the wife of Brigham Young, wrote, "We could breathe more freely and speak with one another upon those things where in God had made us free with less carefulness than we [had] hitherto done." Zina D. Young, another one of Young's wives, agreed. "Here, at length, we could give this introduction ['Woman, this is my husband's wife!'] without fear of reproach, or violation of man-made laws." Historian Richard E. Bennett described Winter Quarters as "a wilderness laboratory, a proving ground where leaders could evaluate the practice" of polygamy.[15]

Young married plural wives before Smith's death. In 1843 he married two wives; in 1844 he married four more. After Smith's death, he married three of Smith's wives following an Old Testament pattern that a brother should marry his deceased brother's wives to raise up seed to honor the dead. Young was not a physical brother, but Young and Smith saw themselves as brothers in a common belief.

After the Mormons arrived in Utah, Young married additional wives. In 1846 he had twelve wives and nine children. In 1857 Young, the territorial leader, had sixteen wives and thirty-eight living children (eight children had died). By the time of his death, Young had had children by sixteen of his twenty-five wives. These numbers do not include thirty other wives to whom he was sealed for eternity.[16]

A frequently asked question is how many wives and children Brigham Young had. Travelers to Utah in the nineteenth century asked Young directly; scholars who have researched his life have tried to count. Jeffrey O. Johnson's article on the subject represents the best attempts. He said that Young had fifty-five wives. Sixteen of these bore Young's fifty-seven children. Emmeline Free Young had ten children; six wives had only one child. His oldest child, Elizabeth Young Ellsworth, was fifty-two, and his youngest, Fannie Young Clayton, was seven when

Young died.

Seven wives divorced Young. The first was in 1846. Mary Woodward had been married to Young for less than a year. He wrote to her, "In answer to your letter of yesterday . . . you may concern yourself discharged from me and my counsel." He added that he would help her and her children from a previ-

Ann Eliza Webb Young

ous marriage if they needed food. In 1851 Mary Ann Clark Powers asked him "to release me from all engagements with you for time and eternity." Young agreed. The Church started recording divorces in 1851; two wives received divorces that year—one in 1853 and one in 1855. In 1873 Ann Eliza Webb, who wrote that she was Young's twenty-seventh wife, received a divorce. The five-year marriage was not recognized by the civil courts, but Young was still ordered to pay $500 a month allowance and $3,000 court costs. He refused and was fined $25 and a day in jail. Webb was excommunicated in 1874 and spent much of her life speaking and publishing about her Mormon polygamous experience.[17]

Public Announcement of Plural Marriage

After Smith's death, there was confusion regarding who should succeed him. Some felt that Joseph Smith's young son, Joseph Smith III, should be the next leader. Others felt that the leader of the Council of Twelve, Brigham Young, should replace Smith. Before Smith's death, he had considered moving west to escape his enemies. Young followed Smith's plan and took his followers to the Great Basin. Once they were isolated, Young decided to admit the practice of polygamy. Orson

Orson Pratt

Pratt, an apostle, made a public announcement in 1852.

Journalist Hosea Stout recalled: "Orson Pratt preached today on the subject of polygamy or plurality of wives as believed and practiced by the Latter Day Saints. In the afternoon the Revelation on the subject given to Joseph Smith . . . was publicly read for the first time to come when we could publickly declare the . . . greatest principles of our holy religion."[18]

Besides making the announcement, Pratt also explained some of the reasons that the Latter-day Saints practiced polygamy. The main reason was that it was a commandment from God. He explained that Joseph Smith and his successors "held the keys" for revelation from God. By accepting plural marriage, couples "could attain their exaltation" and "be counted worthy to hold the scepter of power over a numerous progeny."

Annie Richardson Johnson, a child of a polygamous family, summarized years later: "Like Joseph Smith, polygamists had sealed their testimony, not only with their blood but with the power of acceptance when the principle of Plural Marriage was revealed. . . . This extreme test was possible only because they knew that theirs was the revealed Church of Jesus Christ directed by his priesthood and by revelation, and that blessings came through daily obedience to its principles."[19]

Pratt continued his support of polygamy by arguing that it fulfilled God's command to Adam and Eve to "multiply and replenish the earth." He asked, "Does it say continue to multiply for a few years, and then the marriage contract must cease. . . . No. When male and female are restored from the fall, they will continue to increase and multiply to all ages of eternity." Polygamy allowed more spirits to come to earth via religious homes.[20]

Finally, Pratt argued that monogamy was unnatural. He explained, "Only about one-fifth of the population of the globe . . . believe in the one-wife system; the other four-fifths believe in the doctrine of a plurality of wives . . . and are not so narrow and contract in their minds as some of the nations of Europe and America."

Pratt was correct. In his 1967 *Ethnographic Atlas,* George Peter Murdock pointed out that of 862 societies, nearly 84 percent practiced polygyny (a man married to more than one wife), less than one-tenth of 1 percent practiced polyandry (a woman married to more than one husband), and 16 percent were strictly monogamous. Pratt did not give details, but other scholars have also found examples where Christians encouraged polygamy. According to John Cairncross's *When Polygamy Was Made a Sin*, Martin Luther attacked Catholic celibacy and suggested that Henry VIII of England have two wives at a time. The Catholic Church suggested polygamy after the Thirty Years War with Germany in 1650 to rebuild the population.[21]

Monogamy, according to Pratt, led to "haunts of prostitution, degradation, and misery. . . . Whoredom, adultery, and fornication have cursed the nations of the earth for many generations; . . . but they must be entirely done away with from those who call themselves the people of God." He insisted that prostitution could be eliminated "in the way the Lord devised in ancient times; that is, by giving to his faithful servants a plurality of wives by which a numerous and faithful posterity can be raised up, and taught in the principles of righteousness and truth."[22]

Pratt listed official reasons for the Mormon practice of polygamy. Nearly all of them were religious. However, the

Mormons came up with other reasons to justify the practice. Some of them were developed at the time; others were created by descendants to explain the practice. One common belief was that there was a shortage of men. Some Mormons claimed that the men were killed in war—the Mexican War or the Indian wars. While Brigham Young accepted an invitation by the U.S. government to form a Mormon Battalion, the group did not fight any battles. And the "wars" between Mormons and Native Americans in Utah were more like raids than wars, and few Mormons were killed. There was a belief that more women than men joined the Church, but census studies show that there were about equal numbers of men and women in Utah.

So if there were enough men, another concern was that the women needed to marry "good" men, men who practiced the Mormon religion. Carrie C. Smith, who lived in Cardston, Alberta, Canada, said that without polygamy and with many young men "partaking of the habits of the world, what were the pure daughters of Israel going to do for good LDS husbands?"

"Good" could also refer to those who were established and could provide a good living. Ursula Rich Cole, the daughter of William Lyman Rich and his first wife, Eliza Amelia Pomeroy, said of her father's marriage to a second wife: "I guess Mira was surprised when father asked her, but she believed in the Principle. And besides father was a good provider and by that time had accumulated property. Any girl would take a successful bishop in preference to a single man with nothing."[23]

Others argued that men accepted polygamy for sexual reasons. Men were not allowed to have intercourse when a woman was pregnant or nursing, so polygamy provided a way to have sexual relations while still within a marriage relationship. This motive is hard to document because Americans rarely discussed sex. In the 1930s James Hulett tried to ask Mormons about their sexual reasons for accepting polygamy. The surviving husbands and wives told him that sexual intercourse was only for procreation. Other than that, he did not receive any answers to his questions about sex.

J. W. Wilson, a monogamist leader in the Mormon Colonies in Mexico, wrote, "Polygamy is a true principle . . . but men did not live it as they should have done. . . . I talked to a man who had married a number of wives. I asked him why he did it and he said . . . that all of his marriages were due to inspiration. . . . I asked him that now as he grew older and his desires were dying if he had inspirations to marry and he said no, that he had no more inspirations." Wilson concluded, "That was the reason polygamy could not be lived, men believed it because of their lustful desires."[24]

With hindsight, some historians have argued that polygamy was a way to focus more attention on the Church than on the family. Lawrence Foster wrote, "By partially breaking down exclusive bonds between husband and wife and by undercutting intense emotional involvement in family affairs in favor of Church business, polygamy may well have contributed significantly both to the success of the long-range centralized plans set in motion at this time and to the rapid and efficient establishment of religious and communal order."[25] The theory works in retrospect, but there are no records at the time that support the idea.

Those who question the practice of polygamy by the LDS Church sometimes refer to verses from the Book of Mormon in which a prophet named Jacob condemned the men of his time for marrying plural wives. Jacob 2:27–30 reads: "Wherefore, my brethren, hear me, and hearken to the word of the Lord: For there shall not any man among you have save it be one wife; and concubines he shall have none; for I, the Lord

God, delight in the chastity of women. And whoredoms are an abomination before me; thus saith the Lord of Hosts. Wherefore, this people shall keep my commandments, saith the Lord of Hosts, or cursed be the land for their sakes."

Mormon theologians point out that those using this quote to condemn Mormon polygamy fail to continue to read verse 30, which says, "For if I will, saith the Lord of Lords, raise up seed unto me, I will command my people; otherwise they shall hearken unto these things."

Latter-day Saints occasionally come up with other possibilities. Some say that the restoration of the gospel was not complete until all the practices from the Old Testament were practiced, if only for a short time. BYU English professor Eugene England wrote an essay on why there will be monogamy in heaven. He argued that polygamy was an Abrahamic sacrifice that the Latter-day Saints needed to experience to show their faith. But it would not continue in the next life. [26]

The only answer that makes sense to me is that Mormon polygamists believed that the marriage pattern was a commandment from God. They would be unable to reach the highest exaltation with God in the next life unless they obeyed this higher law. Sociologist Kimball Young agreed:

"While we examine the wide range of motives which appear in our records of polygamous families, we note that there is nearly always a basic faith in the principle of plurality of wives. . . . It was thought to have divine sanction and to promise rewards here and in the hereafter."

Young was not satisfied with that conclusion though, so he added, "Secondary motives . . . emerged, but since deeper motives are hidden below the surface of our daily habits, it is not expected that writers of personal documents or informants in interviews would be able to expose their deeper desires in these matters."[27]

I believe accepting polygamy was of God was the deepest motive.

Notes

1.   Clyde J. Williams, *The Teachings of Lorenzo Snow* (Salt Lake City: Deseret Book, 1984), 1 as cited at www.lds.org/churchhistory/presidents/controllers/ potcController.jsp?leader=5&topic=quotes

2.   BYU Devotional, January 14, 2003.

3.   60 Minutes, May 13, 2007, http://60minutes.yahoo. com/segment/67/mitt_romney.

4.   Genesis 22:16–18; Exodus 20:13; Numbers 31:1–13, King James Version of Holy Bible.

5.   BYU Devotional, May 22, 2007.

6.   In W. H. Auden, *The Living Thoughts of Kierkegaard* (Bloomington, Ind.: Indiana University Press, 1971), 109–10.

7.   Bruce R. McConkie, *The Millennial Messiah* (Salt Lake City: Deseret Book, 1982), 175.

8.   Dallin H. Oaks, "Nourishing the Spirit," *Ensign*, December 1998, 7.

9.   Information in this section comes from Jessie L. Embry, *Mormon Polygamous Families: Life in the Principle* (Salt Lake City: University of Utah Press, 1987), 6.

10.   Richard L. Bushman, *Joseph Smith: Rough Stone Rolling* (New York: Alfred A. Knopf, 2005), 491.

11.   Lawrence Foster, *Religion and Sexuality: the Shakers, the Mormons, and the Oneida Community* (Urbana, Ill.: University of Illinois Press, 1981), 125–26.

12.   Fawn McKay Brodie, *No Man Knows My History: the Life of Joseph Smith, the Mormon Prophet* (New York: Alfred A. Knopf, 1945), 297.

13.   William D. Morain, *The Sword of Laban: Joseph Smith, Jr. and the Dissociated Mind* (Washington, D.C.: American Psychiatric Press, 1998).

14.   Todd Compton, *In Sacred Loneliness: the Plural Wives of Joseph Smith* (Salt Lake City: Signature Books, 1996).

15.   Richard E. Bennett, *Mormons at the Missouri, 1846–1853: "And Should We Die"* (Norman, Okla.: University of Oklahoma Press, 1987), 194–95.

16.   Leonard J. Arrington, *Brigham Young: American Moses* (New York: Alfred A. Knopf, 1985), 121, 323, 421.

17.   Jeffrey O. Johnson, "Defining 'Wife': The Brigham Young Households," *Dialogue: A Journal of Mormon Thought* 20:3 (1987): 62–63.

18.   Jessie L. Embry, *Mormon Polygamous Families: Life in the Principle* (Salt Lake City: University of Utah Press, 1987), 7–8.

19.   Ibid., 42.

20.   Ibid., 44.

21.   Ibid., 46, 3–5.

22.   Ibid., 46.

23.   Ibid., 47–52.

24.   Ibid.

25.   Foster, *Religion and Sexuality,* 211.

26.   Brent Corcoran, *Multiply and Replenish: Mormon Essays on Sex and* Family (Salt Lake City: Signature Books, 1994). Eugene England, "Fidelity, Polygamy, and Celestial Marriage, Brent Corcoran, ed., *Multiply and Replenish: Mormon Essays on Sex and Family* (Salt Lake City: Signature Books, 1994), 103-22.

27.   Kimball Young, *Isn't One Wife Enough?* (New York: Henry Holt & Co., 1954), 118–19.

Reactions to Polygamy

U.S. Government Opposition to Polygamy[1]

Just two years after the announcement that Mormons were practicing polygamy, American politicians reacted against it. In 1854 the Republican Party called for the elimination of "the twin relics of barbarism"—polygamy and slavery. After the Civil War started, Rep. Justin S. Morrill of Vermont introduced legislation to prohibit plural marriage in the territories. President Abraham Lincoln signed the bill in 1862, but reportedly said, "You tell Brigham Young if he will leave me alone, I'll leave him alone." During the Civil War, the federal government made no effort to enforce the new law.

In 1867, after the Civil War, the Utah Territorial Legislature asked Congress to repeal the Morrill Act. This sent up a red flag to Congress, and rather than repealing the act, the House of Representative and Senate decided to strengthen the law. The Poland Act, passed in 1874, provided enforcement for the Morrill Act. It put the United States attorney and marshal assigned to Utah in charge of enforcing the law. It limited the control of the probate courts, which had been an extension of the Mormon Church. The federal government appointed commissioners to assist the federally appointed Territorial Supreme Court. When the Poland Act failed to end Mormon polygamy, Congress continued to introduce other bills to control the Mormons. Not all these bills passed, but those that did forced the Mormons to react.

Women and Defense of Polygamy

To those outside the Mormon Church, polygamy was an example of a patriarchal order's attempt to control women. The common view was that the women were oppressed and denied rights. Mormon women, on the other hand, argued that plural marriage was positive. It gave them greater freedom and more opportunities. When the federal government attempted to pass the Cullom Act to strength the Morrill law, Mormon women gathered to protest.

Eliza R. Snow pointed out that the outside world believed that Mormon women were "in a state of vassalage." Snow declared, "What nonsense." She was joined by six thousand women who expressed the same view at a January 13, 1870, meeting. The Church-owned newspaper, the *Deseret News,* declared that the law would take away the "dearest" of women's rights, "the right to choose a husband."

To show that women were not oppressed, the Utah Territorial Legislature voted to give females the vote in 1870. Brigham Young supported the legislation, and Utah women were granted suffrage. Utah was the second territory to grant the vote (Wyoming was the first), but Utah women were the first to cast their vote. While the Mormons saw the vote as a way to show that women had rights, non-Mormons believed that Mormon women would use the vote to eliminate polygamy.[2]

Testing the Law and More Legislation[3]

Mormons argued that they had the right to practice polygamy because the First Amendment in the Bill of Rights to the U.S Constitution guaranteed freedom of religion. George Reynolds, one of Brigham Young's secretaries, agreed to a trial case. In 1879 the Supreme Court heard the case and upheld the Morrill Act. The federal judges argued, "Laws are made for the government of actions, and while they cannot interfere with mere religious beliefs and opinions, they may with practices."

George Reynolds

John Taylor, who had replaced Young (who died in 1877) as president of the Church, said in response to the ruling: "We are between the hands of God and the hands of the Government of the United States. God has . . . commanded us to enter into these covenants with each other. . . . I know they are true, . . . and all the edicts and laws of Congress and legislators and decisions of courts could not change my opinion."

Instead of solving concerns about polygamy, the Reynolds case brought more public opposition to the Mormons. Many Americans petitioned Congress to control Mormon polygamy in 1881 and 1882. In response, Congress passed the Edmunds Act in 1882. George F. Edmunds, a Vermont Republican, introduced a bill that added amendments to the Morrill Act. The new law made polygamy a felony that carried a penalty of five years in jail and a fine of five hundred dollars. Unlawful cohabitation, which required proof only that a man and woman were living together and did not require proof of a secret marriage ceremony, remained a misdemeanor with a six-month jail sentence and a fine of three hundred dollars. To vote, Mormons had to take an oath that they did not practice polygamy. In 1884 the U.S. Supreme Court allowed the disenfranchisement of plural husbands but declared the test oath unconstitutional.

The law also took the vote away from women married to polygamous husbands.

When the Edmunds Act failed to stop Mormon polygamy, Congress passed the Edmunds-Tucker Act in 1887 with even more restrictions. It required plural wives to testify against their husbands, dissolved an emigration fund, eliminated a military unit, and made arrangements to put all Church property into receivership. Women completely lost the vote whether they lived in plural relations or not. Members of Congress saw that their hope that the women's vote would eliminate polygamy had not happened.

Attacks on polygamy were not limited to Utah. The Idaho legislation passed laws that required residents to take a test oath that they did not believe in polygamy before they could vote. Mormons challenged the law but the Idaho Territorial Supreme Court upheld the oath. In 1890 the U.S. Supreme Court in Davis v. Beason agreed that the law was constitutional. According to historian E. Leo Lyman, "The way was cleared for anti-polygamy advocates to enact similar legislation nationwide."[4]

Mormons' Reaction to the Legislation[5]

Despite federal laws against polygamy, the Mormons did not give up the practice. They believed that God had asked them to marry plural wives and obeying God was more important than obeying the law. Brigham Young's successors John Taylor and Wilford Woodruff affirmed that polygamy was the will of God. On January 9, 1870, Woodruff spoke at the Tabernacle and declared, "Now which will we obey, God or Congress?" Those attending the meeting proclaimed, "We will obey God."[6]

To avoid arrest, Church leaders and other polygamists escaped federal marshals by hiding; by going to other territories, states, or countries; or by having their wives move or stay out of sight.

Some polygamists simply hid near their homes. Edwin Nelson Austin built a secret room in the duplex that his two families shared. John Snyder "somehow or other . . . was able to find out when the marshals were coming over through" Bear Lake, Idaho. He always showed up in the area to warn, "The marshals are coming." Austin and four or five other polygamists hid in the Austin home.

Another way to escape the marshals was to move. The federal marshals assigned to Utah could not arrest polygamists in other territories or states. So Mormons moved to western Wyoming, where territorial officials encouraged settlement. Mormons also went to northern Arizona or southern Idaho. When the husband did not move, wives left and hid in the "underground"—a term taken from the slavery underground before the Civil War. Especially when a wife was pregnant, she needed to avoid the marshals because federal laws could require her to testify against her husband.

Ann Amelia Chamberlain Esplin recalled that her brother was born in Pipe Springs, Arizona, just a few miles from the Utah State line. "The authorities came down and if they had an order to arrest a Utah man and he was in Arizona, why it was no good. So when women would get pregnant, they'd take them to Pipe Springs. . . . They finally dubbed it as the lambing ground for the polygamists."

An even better way to escape the marshals was to move to another country. Some men and women went to Europe. Martha Hughes Cannon, the fourth wife of Angus Munn Cannon, president of the Salt Lake City Stake, provides one example. Martha, a trained doctor, hid in Centerville, Utah, just north of Salt Lake City after she had a daughter. But then she went to England to escape the marshals.[7]

In 1886 B. H. Roberts, who had returned from serving in the Southern States Mission, was working for the *Salt Lake Herald,* a non-Mormon newspaper. On December 5, he was arrested and charged with unlawful cohabitation with Sarah Louis Roberts and Celia Dibble. Fearing that the investigation would show that Roberts did indeed have two wives, Church leaders suggested that Roberts go to England to edit the *Millennial Star,* a Mormon publication. Roberts jumped bail and traveled across the United States and then to England under an assumed name.

Eventually he wrote to Apostle Joseph F. Smith, "I would prefer to return home, plead guilty to the charge, go to prison for the six months, after which live apart from both families and go to work to provide for them." As a result, in September 1888 Roberts received a release from his call. He returned home to a job as editor of the Church's young men magazine, the *Contributor,* and a call to serve as a member of the First Council of Seventy, a general Church office.[8]

But it was not necessary to cross an ocean to go to another country. An easier way was to go to Canada or Mexico. In 1885 Church president John Taylor explored the states of Sonora and Chihuahua in northern Mexico. Based on his recommendations, about four hundred colonists moved south. The Mormons established six communities in Chihuahua and two in Sonora. Technically polygamy was against the law in Mexico, but Mexican president Porfirio Diaz wanted to encourage American settlers. He reportedly said he did not care how many horses pulled a cart, meaning that he did not care how many wives the Mormon men had. He appreciated their farming abilities.

While Mexico worked as a settlement, some Mormons looked to Canada, where the Anglo traditions and language matched their own. In 1886 Charles Card, stake president in Cache Valley on the northern Utah border, discussed his concerns about polygamy with President Taylor. Taylor told him, "I have always found justice under the British flag." Card looked in British Columbia but eventually selected land just over the Canadian border in Alberta.

Card and Mormon Apostles Francis M. Lyman and John W. Taylor went to Ottawa to ask Prime Minister John A. Macdonald if they could bring their plural wives to the country. They argued that others in the British Empire practiced polygamy. Macdonald was not convinced and denied the request, so the Mormon settlers decided to bring only one wife to Canada. They had essentially two legal wives—one who lived in Canada and one who resided in the United States.

Despite their best efforts to escape U.S. marshals, some polygamists were arrested and served time in jail. George Q. Cannon, a member of the First Presidency, spent five months in the territorial prison in Sugarhouse, now a suburb of Salt Lake City. Other men went to federal penitentiaries. When B. H. Roberts returned from England, he was eventually ar-

Mormon polygamists in prison. George Q. Cannon is in the middle with the beard.

rested and sentenced for unlawful cohabitation. The usual penalty was six months in jail and a three hundred dollar fine. Roberts was given four months and fined two hundred dollars. Because he took a "pauper's oath" that he could not pay the two hundred dollars, he was given an additional month in jail. He served four months and nine days, from May 1 to September 10, 1889. His sentence was shortened for good behavior. Roberts was sent to the Castle Prison at the mouth of Parley's Canyon.[9]

The Manifesto[10]

The situation worsened when Isaac N. Struble, a representative from Iowa, and Shelby M. Cullom, a senator from Illinois, introduced legislation to create an even stricter law against polygamy. Church leaders worked with lobbyists to prevent the bill from passing. The pressure included key Church leaders like George Q. Cannon threatening to switch their support from the Republican Party. It also included talk that President Wilford Woodruff might announce plans to eliminate polygamy. Woodruff met with lobbyists and government officials and decided that he needed to do something about the practice of polygamy to preserve the Church.[11]

After much prayer and discussion, Woodruff finally wrote in his journal on September 25, 1890, "I have arrived at a point in the history of the Church of Jesus Christ of Latter-day Saints where I am under the necessity of acting for the temporal salvation of the Church." The next day he issued a press release, referred to as the Manifesto. He wrote, "I publicly declare that my advice to the Latter-day Saints is to refrain from contracting any marriages forbidden by the law of the land." Federal officials required a vote of the Church membership, so on October 6, 1890, those attending a general conference approved the Manifesto.

Woodruff's counselor George Q. Cannon justified the Manifesto by referring to a time when Joseph Smith was commanded to build a temple in Missouri. The tensions with the neighbors in Jackson County made that impossible, and Smith reported a revelation that relieved the Mormons of the responsibility. Woodruff made similar statements. He said that he would have defended polygamy to the end because it was not "for me to have taken a stand in anything which is not pleasing in the sight of God, or before the heavens. I would rather have gone out and been shot." But he recognized that he could not continue to go against the laws of the United States. "The Lord has given us commandments concerning many things and we have carried them out as far as we could, but when we cannot do it, we are justified. The Lord does not require at our hands things that we cannot do."[12]

Effects of the Manifesto[13]

Did the Manifesto end the discussion of Mormon polygamy? No. There were still a lot of unanswered questions. Did the Manifesto apply only to new marriages? What happened to plural families? Were men expected to abandon their wives? President Woodruff told Church members that they should care for their wives. His counselor George Q. Cannon said, "A man who will act the coward and shield himself behind the Manifesto by deserting his plural wives should be damned."

At the same time Woodruff appeared before Judge Charles F. Loofbourow to determine plans for the return of Church property. When the judge asked if the Manifesto referred to existing marriages, and Woodruff replied, "I intended the proclamation to cover the ground, to keep the law." Later he told Church leaders that "he was placed in such a position on the witness stand that he could not answer other than he did. Yet any man who deserts and neglects his wives or children because of the Manifesto, shall be handled [tried] on his [membership]."

The U. S. Congress and presidents cited polygamy and political control as the reasons that Utah remained a territory. With the elimination of polygamy and the Church political party, Utah finally became a state in 1896. One of the conditions required for statehood was that the Utah State Constitution had to outlaw polygamy. That provision is still in the constitution. The constitutional convention debated whether women should be given the vote, and despite opposition, the constitution also included women's suffrage. Mormons celebrated the increased control that statehood brought.

Did Mormon Polygamy End in 1890?[14]

The Manifesto did not eliminate all new plural marriages or all cohabitation. George Q. Cannon explained in an 1899 interview that if a man's wife was barren he "might go to Canada and marry another wife. He would not be violating our laws, and would not be in danger of prosecution unless the first wife should follow him there from Utah and prefer a charge of bigamy against him. He might go to Mexico and have a religious ceremony uniting him to another that would not violate our law."

Being barren was not the only reason that men married plural wives. Some men took wives they had planned to marry before the Manifesto. Others felt that the action was only political, and if men and women were careful they could still marry in polygamy.

Wilford Woodruff and his successor, Lorenzo Snow, avoided discussing plural marriages, but they authorized Cannon to deal with plural marriages on a case-by-case basis. When couples came to him and asked if they could marry, he told some to go to Mexico, where Anthony W. Ivins, who later became a counselor to Church president Heber J. Grant, would perform a ceremony. Ivins performed other plural marriages for those already in Mexico.

Joseph C. Bentley shows the variety of marriages that occurred in Mexico. Bentley lived in St. George and trained his first wife, Margaret (Maggie) Ivins, as a telegraph operator.

Joseph C. Bentley

They married in 1886 when Joseph was twenty-seven and Maggie was eighteen. At the time he told Maggie that he hoped to practice polygamy, and she told him that she expected that he would accept plural marriage. Maggie thought that her cousin Gladys Woodsmansee of Salt Lake City would be a good choice for a second wife. Joseph courted her, and they planned to marry. But it was after the Manifesto. The family tradition is that Joseph asked Church leaders several times if he could marry Gladys. He was referred to Cannon, who suggested that he move to Mexico. So Maggie and Joseph moved there in 1894. Gladys came to visit, and the marriage was performed. Joseph was thirty-five, and Gladys was twenty-nine. They had five children.

Joseph became a leader in the Mormon town of Colonia Juarez. He was the bishop, the ward leader, and a prominent businessman. One of his partners, Ernest Leander Taylor, had a daughter named Maud who was known for her red hair and running ability. Joseph was attracted to her, and her father encouraged him. Maud was embarrassed by Joseph's attention, but she finally agreed to date him. They were married in 1901 when Joseph was forty-two and Maud was sixteen. They had eight children.

Apostles also performed marriages in the United States. Matthias Cowley (who was later disfellowshipped for performing marriages after 1904) explained, "I was never instructed to go to a foreign land to perform these marriages. President Cannon told me to do these things or I would have never done it."

Arthur William Hart, an attorney in Preston, Idaho, married his first wife, Ada Doney Lowe, on August 22, 1900. He married a second wife, Evadyna Henderson, on August 21, 1903.

Not only did Church leaders perform new polygamous marriages after the 1890 Manifesto, but they also continued to live with their plural wives. The federal government and the courts chose to ignore these violations, expecting the practice to die out. But Congress opposed Mormons being elected to the House of Representatives or the Senate. B. H. Roberts was elected to the House in 1899, but because he was a polygamist, Congress refused to let him take a seat. Roberts had served prison time for polygamy, but he married another wife, Margaret Shipp, after he was released. A few months after the Manifesto was issued, Roberts's wife Celia had twins. Roberts reported, "I will not abandon these women even if the Church tells me to."

While most Americans felt that Roberts should not be allowed to serve in Congress, Charles W. Elliot, president of Harvard University, and Susan B. Anthony, the women's suffrage leader, felt that the issue was constitutional and not emotional. Elliot said, "If Mr. Roberts was a polygamist before polygamy became illegal in the territory, I think he was absolutely right in continuing to maintain his wives and their children. . . . In my judgment, that was the only proper thing for a Mormon to do. I should not consider him an unsuitable member of Congress." Anthony had urged the women of Utah not to vote for Roberts, but after his election, she declared, "Congress has not the power to seat or unseat a man. He was elected by the voters from his State, and the Constitution does not give Congress the power to throw him out."[15]

Initially Roberts took his seat in Congress and voted for the speaker of the House. The next day he was forced to defend his right to serve. After a debate, the House voted not to seat Roberts. A committee met to discuss the issue, and Roberts was allowed to defend himself. The committee voted 7 to 2 to exclude Roberts, and the House voted 244 against him and 50 for him, with 36 abstaining.

Despite the fact that he was not allowed to take his seat in the House, Roberts was listed in the *Who's Who in America* as "an ex-Congressman." A quarter century later, Roberts commented that he would have liked to have been in Congress. Some senators and representatives felt that he would have been a strong representative, but George Q. Cannon felt that Roberts added to the pressure on the Mormons.[16] Roberts remained a loyal American and served as a chaplain for the Utah National Guard during World War I.

Polygamy was still an issue in 1904 when Reed Smoot, a monogamist apostle, was elected by the Utah State Legislature to the U.S. Senate. The Senate conducted a lengthy investigation on whether Smoot should be allowed to serve. Those opposed felt that he owed his allegiance to the LDS Church and could not support the Constitution. Those who supported him, including U.S. President Theodore Roosevelt, felt that Smoot should serve because he had been elected.

To determine the case, the Senate asked Church president Joseph F. Smith, Joseph Smith's nephew, to testify. President Smith gave carefully guarded answers but admitted that he had continued to cohabit with his plural wives. However, he recognized that the Church needed to make a strong statement to end the plural marriage discussion. On April 7, 1904, he presented to Church members at general conference what historians refer to as the Second Manifesto. President Woodruff's Manifesto had eliminated marriages "contrary to the laws of the land" but gave no penalty for violators. Smith added punishment.

"If any officer or member of the church shall assume to solemnize or enter into such marriage he will be deemed in transgression against the church and will be liable to be dealt with according to the rules and regulations thereof and excommunicated therefrom."[17]

Even after this statement, Matthias Cowley and John W. Taylor, two apostles, continued to perform plural marriages and marry additional wives. As a result, in 1911 Cowley was disfellowshipped (a less severe punishment than excommunication), and Taylor was excommunicated. In 1909 a group of Church leaders met to discuss post-Manifesto marriages. By 1910 the Church established a new policy. Those married after 1904 were excommunicated. Those married between 1890 and 1904 were called in and asked not to hold positions in the Church in which members would have to sustain them.[18]

The Church officially ended plural marriages in 1904, but many plural wives and husbands continued to cohabit until their deaths. Edward Christian Eyring and his two wives, sisters Caroline Romney Eyring and Emma Romney Eyring, provide an interesting example. Edward's father, Henry Eyring, moved to Mexico in 1887 to escape the federal marshals. He was successful and asked Edward to join him in 1889. Edward married his first wife, Caroline, in 1893. He later wrote, "I decided to try and enter the holy order of plural marriage, so with the help of my wife, I was able to woo my wife's sister Emma and after considerable persuasion married her in November 1903."

Edward recalled his years in Mexico as "wonderful," but

they did not last. During the Mexican Revolution, the Mormons were forced to take sides or leave the country. The women and children left Mexico first in 1912; later the men followed. A few, like Joseph C. Bentley, elected to return to Mexico as soon as possible to avoid the polygamy issue. Others, like Edward Christian Eyring and his families, decided to stay in the United States. They moved to Arizona. Caroline died on April 19, 1954. Just before she passed away, she told her children that she was glad that Emma and Edward would now have some time together alone. Edward and Emma did not live long after her. Edward died on April 13, 1957, and Emma passed away a few months later, on December 18.[19]

Other Churches Based on Joseph Smith, Jr.'s Teachings

Reorganized Church of Jesus Christ of Latter Day Saints (Community of Christ)

Not all those who believed in Joseph Smith moved west with Brigham Young and supported the Mormon practice of plural marriage. In the 1860s a group that believed in Smith's visions but did not support Brigham Young asked Smith's oldest son, Joseph Smith III, to become their leader. Emma Smith, Joseph's first wife, avoided the issue. She married Lewis Bidamon and stayed away from those who followed her husband's teachings. But when Joseph Smith III felt a call to accept a splinter group's offer to lead them, she followed him. The group formed the Reorganized Church of Jesus Christ of Latter Day Saints.

RLDS Church members focused much of their attention on what they were not in the early years. They were not the Mormons in Utah, and they did not practice polygamy. Those who approached Joseph Smith III about starting a new church based on his father's teachings condemned polygamy. For example, Zenos Gurley Sr. recorded an experience he had in the early 1850s in which he reported that God told him, "Polygamy is an abomination in the sight of the Lord God; it is not of me; I abhor it."

Joseph Smith III also disagreed with polygamy. He believed that his father was a good man. Good men do not practice polygamy; therefore, his father did not practice polygamy. Joseph III used these arguments as he attempted to show that his church was the true successor of his father's church. He served missions to Utah in the 1870s to try to convert the "Brighamites" (the followers of Brigham Young).

According to a biography on Joseph Smith III, by historian Roger D. Launius, opposition to polygamy was "one of the few questions upon which most church members agreed during the earliest years of the Reorganized Church." Few of them knew that Joseph Smith had taken additional wives. As with other doctrines of his father that Joseph Smith III disagreed with, Joseph III avoided them as long as those who knew his father were alive. But after they had died, he spoke out against those doctrines.[20]

Joseph Smith III frequently voiced his opposition to polygamy. He went to Washington, D.C., to discuss the Utah Mormons. There was talk at one time that Smith would become the governor of the Utah Territory. That did not happen. When the LDS Church did away with polygamy, Joseph III believed it was the right move. Members of Congress asked him to testify against seating Reed Smoot, but he told them, "It would be a travesty to deny Smoot his legally acquired seat in Congress."

Launius argues that Joseph III could make this statement because his church had grown, the Mormons had given up polygamy, and he and his people had matured.[21] The RLDS Church leader no longer had to prove his church was based on opposition to polygamy.

The RLDS Church, now known as the Community of

Christ, has moved from its reactionary beginnings and is becoming a mainline religion that follows many trends in modern-day Christianity. The church now ordains women and focuses on what it shares with other religions. Many of its church leaders and members downplay the Book of Mormon and Joseph Smith's revelations. They strive to be a prophetic people and accept all people. Like The Church of Jesus Christ of Latter-day Saints and some evangelical churches, the Community of Christ is growing rapidly in third-world countries. An interesting change of position is that polygamists from other cultures can keep wives that they had before joining the Community of Christ. Those who join the LDS Church cannot be baptized if they are practicing polygamists.

Fundamentalists and Practicing Polygamists

While the RLDS Church denied that Joseph Smith ever practiced polygamy, other dissenters who followed Brigham Young and his successor John Taylor felt that Wilford Woodruff was a fallen prophet when he issued the Manifesto. Taylor married an eighth wife in 1886 and died while still in hiding from federal marshals. According to some groups who continue to practice polygamy, Taylor received a revelation during the time he was hiding that polygamy would continue even if the Church abandoned the practice. He selected a group of men to continue plural marriage. Latter-day Saints, however, do not believe that Taylor passed on authority to others to continue plural marriage. They accept the direction of Taylor's successor, Wilford Woodruff.

Until 1918 those who believed that polygamy should continue remained under the radar in the Mormon Church. However, in 1918, under the administration of new Church president Heber J. Grant, Church leaders, according to attorney Ken Driggs, "made concerted efforts to purge the Church of the most zealous advocates of plural marriage." John W. Woolley, his son Lorin C. Woolley, Israel Barlow, his son John Y. Barlow, and Joseph W. Musser, who later played a role in a fundamentalist movement, were excommunicated.

During the 1920s these men formed a loose association with friends and supporters that continued polygamy. Woolley, who had been a Salt Lake Stake leader and a temple worker, led the group. When he died in 1928, his son Lorin took over and, in 1929, formed a priesthood council. J. Leslie Broadbent succeeded him in 1934, and in 1935 John Y. Barlow took over.

At the same time, Mormon Church leaders continued their crackdown on those who continued to marry plural wives. President Grant spoke out sharply against the practice during the 1920s and 1930s. In 1933 Grant's counselor J. Reuben Clark, an attorney and a relative of the Woolleys, prepared a sixteen-page "Final Manifesto" to be read in all wards. Clark condemned the fundamentalists who continued to hand out literature during general conference. Clark also created a "loyalty oath" that fundamentalist supporters were required to sign, or they would be excommunicated. In 1935 the majority of a small branch in Short Creek, Utah, were excommunicated for not signing the oath. Among them was Leroy S. Johnson, a son of Warren Johnson, whom Brigham Young had called to serve a mission at Lee's Ferry on the Utah-Arizona border.

After the excommunications at Short Creek, Barlow and Joseph W. Musser, another fundamentalist, visited Short Creek. The community became a center for those who continued to practice polygamy. Many so-called fundamentalists moved there. In 1939 Barlow died, and Musser succeeded him. Musser was ill and being treated by Rulon Allred, a naturopath and polygamist. When Musser suggested that Allred succeed him, the priesthood council was divided. After Musser's death in 1954, Allred became the leader of the Salt Lake City group.

Leroy Johnson became the leader of the United Effort Trust in Short Creek, now Colorado City, on the Utah-Arizona border.

These fundamentalist groups faced problems from outside their community. In 1935 the Utah legislation made unlawful cohabitation a felony. That year Arizona arrested some Short Creek residents with the assistance of the LDS Church and tried them. In 1944 the states of Arizona and Utah, with assistance from federal officials, raided the polygamous communities and arrested about fifty people. The largest raid was in 1953 when 27 men from Short Creek were arrested and imprisoned, and 160 children and their mothers were placed in foster care. After the men were released, they returned home. Their wives and children also returned, and the families resumed their polygamous lifestyle.

Johnson died in 1986, and Rulon Jeffs, an accountant from Sandy, Utah, became the head of his group. In 1991 the residents of Colorado City incorporated in Utah as the Fundamentalist Church of Jesus Christ of Latter-day Saints. Jeffs died in 2002. After a power struggle, his son Warren declared that he was the new prophet. Members of the FLDS Church consider themselves part of the LDS Church living within special priesthood groups that continue to live the complete gospel. They believe that the LDS Church president is the head of the corporation but that their group's leader is the head of the priesthood.[22]

Like the early Mormons, those who continue to practice polygamy believe that they are following God's commandments. If they are forced to choose between obeying God's laws or man's laws, they select God's. Not all polygamists are connected to the Allred or Jeffs groups. Royston Potter, for example, was an independent polygamist who was fired from his job as a Murray City policeman in the 1980s. Potter did not belong to a group; he married plural wives because he felt that he had a separate command from God to do so. He attempted to appeal his case to the U.S. Supreme Court, but the justices refused to revisit the Reynolds ruling.[23]

Other polygamous groups have also formed. In 1990 James Harmston moved to Manti, Utah, and started to teach that The Church of Jesus Christ of Latter-day Saints had abandoned important doctrines that he would reinstate. In 1994 he and fifty families who believed his ideas were excommunicated from the LDS Church and created the True and Living Church of Jesus Christ of the Last Days (TLC). Within three years three hundred followers called Harmston a prophet. In 1998 his church created a website and defined polygamy in the same way that Orson Pratt had in 1852.

The church did not last, however. In 1995 some of Harmston's followers tried to take over. While Harmston prevailed, 30 percent of the church members left. In 1997 a former apostle, one of his wives, and another woman sued the church for money they had given to the church. That same year Manti residents obtained a copy of one of Harmston's sermons. Unlike nineteenth century polygamists who never discussed sex, Harmston said that one of his wives, a teenager, was "the most cuddling little thing that you ever saw in all your life" although she was not a great lover. Harmston and his eight wives were featured in the *New York Times*. If polygamy is against the law in Utah, how did he get away with this open exposure? Harmston explained, "In today's society . . . we find that the liberal government is far more permissive of nontraditional families."[24]

When Elizabeth Smart was kidnapped by a family handyman named Brian Mitchell, some argued that Mitchell believed that Smart had become a plural wife. Others believed that Smart stayed with him because of her belief in polygamy and prophets. While there is absolutely no proof of this (Brian Mitchell still awaits trial for the kidnapping), magazine articles appeared on the subject.

In *Vogue,* Rebecca Johnson published an article in which she quoted Jeff and Joanne Hanks, a couple living in Salt Lake City who had joined Harmston's church. Jeff Hanks had married a seventeen-year-old from a polygamous family as a plural wife, but she left him because he had had surgery and could not father a child. Eventually, the Hanks decided that they disagreed with Harmston and returned to Salt Lake City, leaving not only polygamy but also The Church of Jesus Christ of Latter-day Saints, which they believed had led them along this path. The Hanks said that while Latter-day Saints do not practice polygamy, there is still a sense that it was important and that Smart might have gone with Mitchell because of such a belief. However, most who continue to accept polygamy do not see a connection between Smart's kidnapping and polygamy and refused to talk to Johnson.[25]

Times have changed since the nineteenth century and even since Royston Potter's appeal to the U.S. Supreme Court. The Supreme Court still has not agreed to hear cases that deal with polygamy, and government officials do not go after polygamists for having more than one wife. As with other sexual relationships between consenting adults, government leaders and police do not try to enforce the law. Rather, they find other pretexts for going after polygamists, including the marriage of underage girls and the abuse of the welfare system.

In 2007 Utah attorney general Mark Shurtleff held workshops in St. George. His position was that the state would arrest only those who broke laws other than polygamy. He pointed out that his concerns were for women and children being abused by the current practice of polygamy. Two examples illustrate that concern. FLDS leader Warren Jeffs is awaiting trial for his part in forcing an underage girl to marry an older man. As of July 2007, Tom Green is currently serving prison time for marrying his first wife when she was not of legal age.

Cohabitation continues to be a felony in Utah. The Utah Supreme Court refused to hear Green's appeal, which is based on the vagueness of the state's bigamy law and his claim that he did not know that he was in disobeying the law.

Notes

1. Information in this section comes from Jessie L. Embry, *Mormon Polygamous Families: Life in the Principle* (Salt Lake City: University of Utah Press, 1987), 8–10.

2. Lola Van Wagenen, *Sister-Wives and Suffragists: Polygamy and the Politics of Woman Suffrage, 1870–1896* (Provo, Utah: Joseph Fielding Smith Institute for Latter-day Saint History, 2003).

3. Information from this section comes from Embry, *Mormon Polygamous Families*, 9–10.

4. E. Leo Lyman, "The Political Background of the Woodruff Manifesto," *Dialogue: A Journal of Mormon Thought* 24:3 (1991):21–40.

5. Unless otherwise cited, the information in this section comes from Embry, *Mormon Polygamous Families*, 17–28.

6. B. Carmon Hardy, "Self-Blame and the Manifesto," *Dialogue: A Journal of Mormon Thought* 24:3 (1991): 44.

7. Constance L. Lieber and John Sillito, *Letters from Exile: The Correspondence of Martha Hughes Cannon and Angus M. Cannon, 1886–1888* (Salt Lake City: Signature Books, 1989), xi–xxiv.

8. Truman S. Madsen, *Defender of the Faith: The B. H. Roberts Story* (Salt Lake City: Bookcraft, 1980), 160–81.

9. Madsen, 182–98.

10. Unless otherwise noted, information from this section comes from Embry, *Mormon Polygamous Families*, 12–14.

11. Lyman.

12. Ibid., 34–35.

13. Unless otherwise noted, information from this section comes from Embry, *Mormon Polygamous Families*, 12–14.

14. Information in this section comes from Embry, *Mormon Polygamous Families*, 14–15; 54–55.

15. Madsen, 250.

16. Ibid., 266–70.

17. Embry, *Mormon Polygamous Families,* 15.

18. Ibid., 16–17.

19. Ibid., 26, 61, 75, 81, 100, 115, 118, 129, 173, 188–89.

20. Roger D. Launius, *Joseph Smith III: Pragmatic Prophet* (Urbana: University of Illinois Press, 1988), 190–209.

21. Ibid., 247–72; 298–99.

22. Ken Driggs, "Twentieth-Century Polygamy and Fundamentalist Mormons in Southern Utah," *Dialogue: Journal of Mormon Thought* 24(Winter 1991):44-58. For information on the 1950s raids, see Martha Sonntag Bradley, *Kidnapped from that Land: The Government Raids on the Short Creek Polygamists* (Salt Lake City: University of Utah Press, 1993).

23. Embry, *Mormon Polygamous Families*, xiv.

24. Kathryn M. Daynes, *More Wives than One: Transformation of the Mormon Marriage System, 1840–1910* (Urbana: University of Illinois Press, 2001), 2.

25.   Jessie L. Embry and Ron Shook, "The Perfect Backdrop: Uses of the Bonneville Salt Flats," *Magazine Americana* www.americanpopularculture.com/archive/sports/salt_flats.htm), January 2006.

Characteristics of Mormon Polygamous Families

Those who continue to practice polygamy are not allowed to remain members of The Church of Jesus Christ of Latter-day Saints. President Gordon B. Hinckley explained in 1998:

"I wish to state categorically that this Church has nothing whatever to do with those practicing polygamy. They are not members of this Church. Most of them have never been members. They are in violation of the civil law. They know they are in violation of the law. They are subject to its penalties. The Church, of course, has no jurisdiction whatever in this matter.

"If any of our members are found to be practicing plural marriage, they are excommunicated, the most serious penalty the Church can impose. Not only are those so involved in direct violation of the civil law, they are in violation of the law of this Church. An article of our faith is binding upon us. It states, 'We believe in being subject to kings, presidents, rulers, and magistrates, in obeying, honoring, and sustaining the law' (Article of Faith 1:2). One cannot obey the law and disobey the law at the same time.

"There is no such thing as a 'Mormon Fundamentalist.' It is a contradiction to use the two words together.

More than a century ago God clearly revealed unto His prophet Wilford Woodruff that the practice of plural marriage should be discontinued, which means that it is now against the law of God. Even in countries where civil or religious law allows polygamy, the Church teaches that marriage must be monogamous and does not accept into its membership those practicing plural marriage."[1]

While there are some similarities between how current polygamous families live and those who had LDS Church-sanctioned marriages in the nineteenth century, this chapter will look only at those sanctioned by the LDS Church. These characteristics do not refer to those who continue to live in polygamy and whom The Church of Jesus Christ of Latter-day Saints does not accept as members. This chapter will answer questions such as how widespread was polygamy in the Church during the nineteenth century and what impact did it have on Church members?

Stereotypes

Because polygamy was practiced for such a short period, and no known official records were kept of plural marriages, it is impossible to give definitive answers to demographic questions about Mormon polygamy. But it is possible to show that in certain study groups the stereotypes are not typical examples.

What are the common stereotypes? One is that many plural wives were older women who needed support and were wives in name only. Husbands did not have sexual relationships with them. Another is that there were few eligible women to marry, so Mormon men frequently married fourteen-year-olds. With all stereotypes, some examples fit each story. But there is no evidence that the old maid or young girl scenarios happened frequently.

Still, these extremes often receive the most attention because they are so sensational. Maurine Whipple, who grew up in St. George, Utah, wrote a novel, *The Giant Joshua*, in the 1940s. She claimed that her fictional study was based on her family history, but a careful study of her family history showed few similarities. The main character is a young woman, Clorin-da Agatha (nicknamed Clory), a ward of the Abijah and Bath-sheba family. Abijah was in his forties, and Clory was sixteen.

In the novel, Clory often refers to her husband as Uncle Abijah and his first wife as Aunt 'Sheba. Clory had seen Bath-sheba as a mother figure, and Bethshaba resisted the marriage and the attention that the husband gave Clory. Clory was the third wife; the second wife, Willie, was a widowed immigrant. Whipple managed to include nearly every stereotype one could imagine. Clory even falls in love with her husband's oldest son from his first marriage.

Whipple's novel was not well received by Mormon leaders and was not the bestseller she had hoped for when it was pub-lished, but it has become a well-read and loved novel. When I gave lectures on the history of Mormon polygamy just before my book *Mormon Polygamous Families* was published, people fre-quently asked me if I had read *The Giant Joshua* and then told me it was the best example of polygamy they had ever read. I usu-ally smiled and said yes, I had read the novel—although I had not. When I discovered a first edition among my grandmother's books, I decided to read it. My impression was that Whipple hit on many stereotypes—the beloved younger wife, the jealous first wife, and a second wife who was married because she needed support and may not have had sexual relations.[2]

Theodore Schroeder, an anti-Mormon attorney who lived in Salt Lake City for a short while, referred to another stereo-type. In his *Journal of Urology and Sexiology* article, he argued that Mormons were guilty of incest during the polygamous pe-riod. This claim was repeated frequently in books about abuse and is the topic that the Church public relations department asked me to research. I found some unusual examples. The most bizarre was an uncle who had married his nieces. But in most cases what Schroeder called incest did not involve direct relations. One man married a mother and her daughter from another marriage. But most of the examples were men who married women who were sisters. As in other societies, many Mormon men believed that marrying sisters who grew up in the same household would eliminate some of the conflict that one would expect in a plural household.[3]

Number of Mormon Polygamists

Problems Counting

Perhaps the most difficult question to answer is how many Mormon families were polygamists. Even in societies that permitted polygamy for generations, the majority of families were not polygamists. In those cases, financial considerations and personalities made plural marriage undesirable. Additional factors played a role in the limited number of Mormon men and women who had polygamous marriages. First, many had a hard time accepting a doctrine so different from their previous background and teaching. Second, Mormons were very poor, and a man often struggled to support one family. Third, general Church leaders encouraged local Church leaders to marry plural wives, but there were no direct requests that the rank and file accept polygamy.

The numbers of plural marriages changed over the years. From the 1830s to 1844, only a few men and women even knew about the practice. The number of polygamists increased after the Mormons left Nauvoo, waited in Winter Quarters, Nebraska, and then moved to Utah. But even after the public announcement in 1852, most Mormons chose not to marry plural wives. Church leaders occasionally reminded members of their duty. According to the participants, those called to leadership positions were often told to take another wife. In the late 1860s after the railroad arrived in Utah, Mormon leaders encouraged members to follow Church leaders. During this

Reformation, the number of marriages increased. However, as more laws were passed against polygamy, fewer men risked breaking the law because they feared arrest. By the time the Manifesto was issued, few plural marriages were performed. There were limited polygamous marriages between 1890 and 1904. Men and women had to make a special request of Church leaders to marry in polygamy.[4]

To determine how many Mormons were polygamists and when they married, BYU history professor Kathryn M. Daynes divided a study group of 155 men and 444 wives in Manti, Utah, into three groups: those born before 1852, those born between 1852 and 1869, and those born between 1870 and 1890. She concluded that the first group married in polygamy at the highest rate. The second was higher than the third because the Church stopped plural marriages in Manti after 1890. She summarized that from 1851 to 1870 the number of Mormon polygamous families grew. It stabilized from 1870 to 1880. The peak periods were 1846 (Winter Quarters), 1852 (public announcement), 1856–57 (Reformation), 1868–69 (Railroad), and 1880. Daynes concluded, "In Mormonism's turbulent history either preaching or persecution may explain almost any increase in plural marriage."[5]

Polygamy was also not practiced equally in all communities. Humboldt State geography professor Lowell C. "Ben" Bennion studied the 1880 census and found that the number of polygamists varied by town. In Washington County, Utah, for example almost 40 percent of the families in St. George were polygamists. In Harrisburg/Leeds, in the same county, only 11 percent were. In Kane County, Utah, the figures varied from 10 percent in Rockville to 67 percent in Orderville. In Davis County, Utah, 30 percent of the families in Bountiful were polygamous, while only 5 percent were in South Weber. Larry Logue also researched St. George and found that 30 percent of the men were polygamists in 1870, rising to 33 percent in 1880. Chris Nelson determined that 63 percent of the Mormon men in the Mormon colonies in Mexico practiced polygamy.[6]

Marie Cornwall, Camela Cartwright, and Laga Van Beek looked at three wards in the Salt Lake Valley. In 1860, 44 percent of the men were polygamists. In 1870, 28 percent of the men in Sugarhouse, a suburb of Salt Lake City, had more than one wife. According to Daynes, that same year 36 percent of the men in Manti had plural wives. That number was up from 30 percent in 1860. It dropped to 25 percent in 1880.[7]

Why were there such differences? The higher numbers are easier to explain than the smaller numbers. Those who originally settled St. George responded to a call from Brigham Young to raise cotton in Utah's Dixie. Their efforts were not successful, but they were some of the most faithful and obedient members. They obeyed the command to move, and they accepted polygamy. During the Reformation period, Young and other Church leaders asked members to live a communal lifestyle. Few such communities lasted, but the townspeople of Orderville were successful. Those who went to the Mormon colonies in Mexico went there to escape federal marshals. It was also a place where plural marriages were performed after 1890.[8]

Number of Polygamous Families

So how many Mormon families were polygamists? Several numbers have been suggested. In his *Comprehensive History of the Church*, B. H. Roberts said that only 2 percent of the men were polygamists. Joseph Fielding Smith, an apostle and later Church president in the 1970s, repeated that figure in his Church-approved history, *Essentials in Church History*. That figure is clearly too low. But the problem with numbers is that they can be changed in many ways to get the desired results. So maybe if Roberts and Smith compared the number of men

married to more than one wife to the entire Church membership, they would come up with 2 percent. But only looking at
the number of men does not show the number of women and
children who were part of plural families.

More recent studies have concluded that 10–25 percent of
Mormon families were polygamists. Stanley S. Ivins said about
20 percent. Church historian Leonard J. Arrington and assistant Church historian Davis Bitton said no more than 5 percent of Mormon married men had more than one wife, and
because the majority only had two wives, they estimated 12
percent of Mormon married women practiced polygamy.[9]

Number of Wives

How many wives did Mormon polygamists have? Cartoon-
ists at the time drew pictures of Brigham Young in bed with
many wives. Young's case is unusual. He had many wives, but
in addition, many women asked to be sealed to him during
and after his lifetime. Other men had multiple wives. Heber C.
Kimball, Young's friend and counselor, had forty-three wives
and sixty-five children. A counselor to four Church presidents,
George Q. Cannon had six wives, thirty-four natural children,
and nine adopted children. Can-
non was an editor, political leader, and businessman.[10]

But Young, Kimball, and
Cannon were not typical. In my
study group, 60 percent of the
men had only one plural wife.
Approximately 20 percent had
three wives, and only 10 percent
had four or more wives.[11] My
study, however, represents a later
period of polygamy.

**George Kirkham and
wives**

Kathryn M. Daynes's sample covered a larger period in Manti, but her percentages are similar to mine. She examined how many wives the men had over their lifetimes, including divorced or deceased women. In Manti, 13.3 percent of the men had five or more wives over their lifetimes; 16.7 percent had four; 32.7 percent had three; and 37.3 had two. But these men did not have all these wives at a time since some died. So Daynes also looked at how many living wives the polygamous men had. Over half (56.7 percent) had two wives; 20.7 percent had three, and only 11.3 percent had five or more. Stanley Ivins's figure showed that 66.3 percent had only two wives.[12]

Ages of Plural Husbands and Wives

How old were the husbands and wives who married in polygamy? As previously mentioned, a popular stereotype is that plural wives were older women who did not have anyone to support them. In an age when women often had to depend on men for support, single women struggled. Nels Anderson, a sociologist who studied Mormons in St. George, argued that most plural wives were immigrants who came to Utah as "older women, many of them ranging between 25 and 35 years of age. . . . Polygamy was a boon for them." Another stereotype was the opposite of Anderson's. As more men married plural wives, there were not enough women to marry, so men married fourteen-year-old girls.

My research shows that there were older women who became plural wives and there were fourteen-year-old girls who married older men. But they were not the norm. Most husbands were in their early twenties when they married for the first time. Their first wife was in her late teens. Those who married only one additional wife were usually in their early thirties when they took a plural wife. And the second wife was between the ages of seventeen and nineteen years of age. If a man married a third wife, he was usually in his late thirties, and his wife was in her late teens. For those few men who married a fourth wife, the man was usually in his thirties or forties, and the wife was usually in her late teens.

Why were the wives so much younger? Of course, the men might have just been attracted to younger women. Another reason is that the revelation on plural marriage mentioned, "If any man espouse a virgin, and desire to espouse another" (D&C 132:61). That implied that a plural wife should not have been married before. If a man wanted more children (a reason for marriage in Mormon society), a wife's age would be important. According to my sample of Mormon monogamous men married a second time after the death of their first wife, they married a woman sixteen years younger.

An important reason for polygamy was to have children born to Mormon families. Did polygamy increase the number of children? According to my study, plural wives had fewer children than their monogamous counterparts. However, there is a possibility that those women would never have married and never had any children without plural marriage. Sometimes a man took a plural wife because his first wife could not have children. However, in my study the first wives often had more children than the other wives.[13]

Notes

1. Gordon B. Hinckley, "What Are People Asking about Us?" *Ensign*, November 1998, 70.
2. Maurine Whipple, *The Giant Joshua* (Boston: Houghton Mifflin, 1941); "Overworked Stereotypes or Accurate Historical Images: The Images of Polygamy in *Giant Joshua*," *Sunstone* 14 (April 1990): 42–46.

3.   Jessie L. Embry, "Intimate Taboos: Incest and Mormon Polygamy," *Journal of Mormon History* 18 (1992): 93–113.

4.   Stanley S. Ivins, "Notes on Mormon Polygamy," *Utah Historical Quarterly* 35 (Fall 1967): 309–21.

5.   Kathryn M. Daynes, *More Wives than One: Transformation of the Mormon Marriage System, 1840–1910* (Urbana, Ill.: University of Illinois Press, 2001), 103.

6.   Jessie L. Embry, *Mormon Polygamous Families: Life in the Principle* (Salt Lake City: University of Utah Press, 1987), 38–39.

7.   Daynes, 100–101.

8.   Embry, *Mormon Polygamous Families*, 38–39.

9.   Ivins, "Notes on Polygamy," 309–21; Leonard J. Arrington and Davis Bitton, *The Mormon Experience: A History of the Latter-day Saints* (New York: Alfred A. Knopf, 1979), 199. A good question that has not been answered is what percentage of eligible men married in polygamy. Unfortunately, that census research has not been done.

10.   For information on Heber C. Kimball, see Stanley B. Kimball, *Heber C. Kimball: Mormon Patriarch and Pioneer* (Urbana, Ill.: University of Illinois Press, 1981). For information on George Q. Cannon, see Davis Bitton, *George Q. Cannon* (Salt Lake City: Deseret Book, 1999).

11.   Embry, *Mormon Polygamous Families*, 33–34.

12.   Daynes, 129–30.

13.   Embry, *Mormon Polygamous Families*, 34–38.

Ins and Outs of Mormon Polygamy[1]

If so few Mormons practiced polygamy, what men married plural wives? Who had to give consent? Section 132 of the Doctrine and Covenants says that the first wife has to agree. That didn't work with Joseph Smith. Did it work in other cases? Did the Church president have to approve each marriage? As the following examples show, there is no one answer.

The Husband

First, did a leader in the Church have to give permission? Under modern guidelines, a bishop, the head of a congregation; and a stake president, the leader over several congregations, issue a temple recommend for eternal marriages. Did

Ira Eldredge and wives

plural marriages follow the same pattern? Mormon marriages were performed in the Endowment House until the first temples were completed in Utah. Then who could issue temple recommends for plural marriages? Some children of polygamous families say that the permission to marry in their family came from the president of the Church. Others said it came from a local leader.

My study represents a later time period for polygamy, but it does show the variety of ways that men felt that they were inspired to marry plural wives. Of the approximately two hundred men used in my study, seventy-eight of the men or their descendants identified a Church official who asked them to marry in polygamy or who approved the marriage. Most said they received a direct request.

George Lake said President Brigham Young asked him to come to Salt Lake City in 1861 and receive special ordinances in the Endowment House. Lake went and had his wife sealed to her first husband. When Young asked Lake how he was doing, Lake said he was sorry his wife was sealed to another man. Young told him, "You have done your duty my boy and your reward shall be greater. . . . Go to now, and in two weeks be here with two more for yourself." Lake wrote, "I pleaded for a little more time as I wished to make a wise choice, so as not to have to trouble with him for a divorce. This he thought would be a good plan but said not to delay."

President John Taylor said polygamy "was applicable to High Councillors [twelve men who work with the stake president], Bishops, and those counselors and all who preside in Zion and if these officers shall not obey this law, their place shall be filled with men who have obeyed the law." Most general authorities of the Church and many of the bishops and stake presidents practiced polygamy.

There were exceptions. David John recorded in his journal

that in 1884 John Taylor, George Q. Cannon, and Joseph F. Smith discussed "Celestial Marriage saying it was binding on all the Latter-day Saints and no man was entitled to the right of Presiding [as a Church leader] without abiding this law." He claimed that Joseph Smith said that a coward could not enter the practice. He added, "If Bro. Wm W. Cluff and Abraham [sic] Hatch and other leading men had gone into this order 18 months or more ago Zion would today have been in a higher place than now."

Abram Hatch, the stake president, probate judge, and territorial legislator, lived in Heber City, Utah, and was a monogamist. According to William Forman, a bishop in Heber City, Hatch refused to marry a plural wife and said at a local priesthood meeting that it took Wilford Woodruff 40 years to obey the Word of Wisdom (the code of health that does not allow tobacco, coffee, tea, or liquor and was not as strictly enforced in the early Church as it is today), and it would take Hatch that long to live polygamy. Forman was frustrated with what he saw as Hatch's disobedience. He wrote in his journal that Hatch "feels quite important and says he is not going to resign," despite his disobedience relating to plural marriage.

Other leaders were asked by general ecclesiastical leaders or local leaders to accept polygamy. Apostle Marriner W. Merrill asked Andrew Larse Hyer, who lived in Lewiston, Utah, to head the seventies, an office in the priesthood, in his stake and asked him to take another wife. Hyer called it "the hardest decision he ever made in his life." After Merrill came three times, he talked to his wife, Ellen Gilbert Hyer, and she agreed to let him marry again. Andrew married Elizabeth Helen Telford in the Logan Temple in 1885. Ellen and Andrew had fourteen children. Elizabeth and Andrew had eleven children.

A stake president asked James Michael Andersen, who also lived in Lewiston, to marry again because he was well off. He suggested Susan Eliza Stephensen, a twenty-two-year-old "good looking" woman who was not courting anyone. His daughter from his first wife explained, "Father just took that for granted what he should do. I think he accepted it just the same as Mother [Margaret Maria White Andersen]."

Others followed the counsel after hearing someone preach on the subject. Sarah Louise (Sadie) Adams was fourteen when she married twenty-four-year-old Charles Edmund Richardson in the St. George Temple in 1882. Several years later Sadie heard a General Authority preach on polygamy and felt that it was something that was God's command. At the same time Sarah Matilda Rogers, a young woman in the Richardsons's ward, told the bishop she wanted to marry Edmund. When the bishop spoke to Edmund about Sarah, he was confused. He did not love Sarah, and he did not plan on marrying again. Sadie did not share her husband's confusion. She told him, "You know that you should be entering into this principle, and you have no right to deprive that good woman of having a family." Edmund agreed married Sarah in the St. George Temple in 1887 when Edmund was twenty-nine and Sarah was thirty-one. Sarah had three children.

Based on these examples, the authorization to marry in polygamy could come from general or local Church leaders. It could also come from a direct request or listening to a conference talk.

The First Wife

With the request to marry, did the husband have to ask for his first wife's consent? Again, the experience varied. Sometimes the first wife, like Sadie Richardson or Maggie Bentley, encouraged a marriage. But the range of possibilities varied. Some first wives felt pressured to accept their husband's decision to marry again. When John Jacob Walser, of Payson,

Utah, married a second wife, he explained, "My first wife did not like the idea at first. She was upset but she got used to it."

Ann Elizabeth Riter Young complained to George Q. Cannon, first counselor in the First Presidency, that her husband, Seymour Young, could not marry again because she had a child with cerebral palsy and other illnesses. Her daughter, Hortense Young Hammond, explained that her mother knew whom her father was courting. "That broke her heart." But, Hortense continued, "Papa was between the devil and the great deep blue sea" because he felt he was commanded by John Taylor to marry again. When Seymour was called to the First Council of Seventy in 1882, John Taylor told him that he was to "confirm to my law." Seymour put off the marriage for eighteen months until Taylor "commanded" him in the April 1884 conference to enter polygamy "immediately."

Ida Walser Skousen, the wife of James Skousen, knew that he was courting Emma Mortensen. She recalled, "One day I was combing his hair and I said to him, 'Would you marry Emma if I refused consent?' He said that he wouldn't, but the responsibility would be on my head." Ida reflected, "Now I'd be willing to take [the responsibility of him not marrying in polygamy], but I wasn't then."

Second Wives

Polygamy was difficult for a first wife, but it wasn't easy for a woman to agree to be a second or a third wife either. Rosalia Tenney Payne, of Colonia Diaz, Mexico, became the third wife of Edward Payne in 1903. She said she made fun of polygamy until she read the revelation in the Doctrine and Covenants. Then she realized it was a divine principle. When Edward asked her to be a plural wife, her family opposed the marriage, and Rosalia had doubts. "But I finally felt that I was doing the right thing and that assurance never left me."

Some young girls courted older established men. Matilda Peterson said her parents only let her go to dances with old married men because they felt "we could not be saved unless we married in polygamy." Mary Elizabeth Woolley Chamberlain, who grew up in a polygamous household and had her husband-to-be ask all five of his wives for their approval before she agreed to the marriage, wrote a poem about living polygamy. She asked if "the daughters of Zion . . . [will] choose for the right and for God?" Her answer was, "Better marry a man who'd be constant/Though wives he may have more than you. If he is faithful to God and his covenants/Be onward he'll be faithful to you."

Getting out of a Polygamous Marriage[2]

Was it possible to get out of a polygamous marriage? Was divorce a possibility? As has already been mentioned, several of Brigham Young's wives divorced him. Determining the number of divorces is difficult because not all plural marriages were officially recorded. The only way to know about divorces is if there was a court case. And even then it is difficult.

In 1852 the Utah territorial legislature passed a liberal divorce law. "To protect plural marriages," it allowed the Church to keep a registry of marriages rather than the civil courts that did not recognize the extra marriages. The law also gave loose requirements for divorce. As a result, many outsiders came to Utah to end their marriages.

In the 1970s Eugene E. and Bruce L. Campbell had access to Brigham Young's papers and other records in the Historical Department. They determined that Young granted 1,645 divorces. Young was willing to give a divorce, especially if a wife asked for it. But there were several problems with the Campbells's figures. First, they used the 2 percent figure from B. H. Roberts's history. The Campbells's study, however, as well as many others, shows that more than 2 percent of the men had polygamous families. Historian Carol Cornwall Madsen explained that Young granted three-fourths of the 1,645 divorces in the first two decades that he was president. During the last decade of his leadership, the number of divorces dropped by 30 percent while the general Church population grew 65 percent.

In 2001, Historian Kathryn M. Daynes looked at other studies that attempted to determine the number of divorces. Researcher Geraldine Mineau concluded, "For 1870 and 1880 the Utah rate [of divorce] was two to three times higher than the U.S. rate; by 1890 and 1900 the difference had greatly decreased." But Mineau only included civic divorces, not divorces within the Church.

Sociologist Phillip Kunz used family group sheets, which Mormons submit for temple work, to look at divorces between 1844 and 1870. He found that 9 percent of the polygamous men were divorced, while less than 3 percent of the wives were. But family group sheets are problematic because they are submitted by family members who may not know of the divorces. Also, given the eternal nature of temple sealings, sometimes a marriage is dissolved on earth but not for the hereafter.

Daynes found 83 divorces among her study group of 465 plural marriages in Manti, Utah. About 18 percent of the plural marriages ended in divorce. Most of those were not the first wife. She also discovered that 35.1 percent of the 151 polygamous men were divorced one or more times. This figure is high but not as high as the current divorce rate.

Reasons for breaking up a marriage included men or women leaving the Church; government raids of polygamous households; adultery; and not getting along. Lack of financial support was another reason for divorce. As with current divorces, there was not only one pattern. Two examples illustrate the variety.

Edward William Payne married his first wife, Emily Bean, in 1889. After ten years they had no children. When Edward asked if he could marry a plural wife, Emily agreed. He married Lucy Alice Farr in 1899 and Rosalia Tenney in 1903. Eldon, a son of Lucy, said that Emily was in Mexico with the families for a while but then she left. Edward lost track of her, although they were not officially divorced until 1917. Eldon said that later Emily was "kind of wanting to get back in the good graces of the children to see if they would take care of her I think. But we were struggling, just getting started and didn't have anything. We couldn't take care of her." Had she stayed with the family, "we would have taken care of her some way."

Edward Franklin Turley married Annie Martineau Walser, a widow with two children, in Mexico. After the family left Mexico, Edward faced financial struggles. So when the U.S. government offered free passage to anywhere in the United States, Annie left and went to Logan, Utah. When Edward returned to Mexico, Annie got a divorce. Clarence, a son of Edward's first wife, Ida Elizabeth Eyring Turley, said, "I told some of the other children that I never did know why my father and Aunt Annie separated." His sister said she did not feel that she had the right to ask her mother. Clarence believed that maybe she felt that Edward did not "treat" her children from her first marriage "right."

Inheritance Laws[3]

Death also ended plural marriages, at least in this life. Dividing property among all the families required special arrangements because the law did not recognize plural wives, and their children could be seen as illegitimate. The 1852 territorial legislature passed laws to protect these wives and children. While a man could have a will giving his property to whomever he wanted, the law provided for men who died intestate.

"Illegitimate children and their mothers inherit in like manner from the father, whether acknowledged by him or not, provided it shall be made to appear to the satisfaction of the court that he was the father of such illegitimate child or children."

The Morrill Act of 1862 included a clause that voided the inheritance laws. The Edmunds Act of 1882 legitimized all children born before January 1, 1883. Future children of polygamous families were declared illegitimate. The Edmunds-Tucker Act said, "No illegitimate child shall here after be entitled to inherit from his or her father or to receive any distributive share in the estate of his or her father." The Utah state constitution, however, made polygamous children legitimate.

Division of family property created problems in some plural families. Joseph Hodges, the oldest son of National Hodges and his second wife, Anna Weston Hodges, complained about the third family. According to Joseph, his father left property but also debts, which took a long time to settle. William, a son of Louise Weston Hodges, the first wife, said he felt that Joseph favored Charlotte, the third wife, because she had a home and farm in her name. The other two wives, sisters, did not have anything in their names. But Charlotte felt that she was being treated unfairly and took the matter to Church court. Joseph said that the stake presidency "cleared me entirely" for his distribution of the property.

Morris, a son of Charlotte, saw the situation differently. After his father had a stroke, he was proven incompetent. The mills and all his property were divided among the three wives. The wives and older children became part of a family business. Morris thought he was old enough to be a member of the Hodges Land and Livestock and Milling Company. However, the rest of the family did not agree, and he was not a partner. He felt that, as a result, the first two families got more property because they had more family members involved in the business. He then added, "So that was about the only time there was a discord there."

Other families divided their father's estate equally. Even though Annie, the second wife, divorced Edward Franklin Turley, the first wife, Ida, told her sons "she wanted Aunt Annie to have half of the field." Clarence, Ida's son, handled the property for years and shared the profits with his half-brothers and sisters. When he sold it, he paid both his full- and half-brothers and sisters and, he recalled, "They were tickled to death." Dividing property after the death of a parent is always a challenge because not all family members see issues the same. Polygamy added to the stress.

As with all aspects of polygamy, getting in and out of the marriages had no set standards. Determining whether to accept plural marriage was an issue that involved the man, his first wife, and any additional wives. Deciding whether to end a marriage also created concerns. And even when the marriage lasted until death, there were unique concerns on how to divide the property.

Notes

1.   Unless otherwise cited, the material comes from Jessie L. Embry, *Mormon Polygamous Families: Life in the Principle* (Salt Lake City: University of Utah Press, 1987), 53-71.

2.   Ibid., 175–81; Kathryn M. Daynes, *More Wives than One: Transformation of the Mormon Marriage System, 1840–1910* (Urbana, Ill.: University of Illinois Press, 2001), 160–67.

3.   Embry, 182-86.

Polygamy in Practice

Case Studies

Some case studies show the variety of ways that plural families adjusted their lifestyle within the family and over time. These cases show that some families worked remarkably well given the circumstances; at the same time, other families had major problems.

Kimball Young said polygamy was not usually the reason for dissent, but it amplified other problems. Speaking of men who married sisters, Young explained, "When the wives fell into serious conflicts, the matter of being sister or not may have far less to do with [the conflict] than the personality divergence, economic problems and sense of differential treatment by the husband."[1] My research supports that conclusion. The following examples show a family with extreme problems and one that the children believed worked well.

William Hendricks Roskelley

William Hendricks Roskelley was born in 1866 in Smithfield, Utah. His father, Samuel Roskelley, had plural wives. Based on his example, William wanted to live plural marriage. He married his first wife, his childhood sweetheart, Margaret Ann Wildman, on March 10, 1886. Margaret was born in Norwood, Ontario, in 1866. Her family did not have a tradition of plural marriage. On January 3, 1888, William married his second wife, Margaret's sister, Agnes Wildman. Like William, Agnes was born in Smithfield. She was four years younger than Margaret. Margaret eventually had twelve children; Agnes had seven children, four of whom survived into early childhood.

Because Agnes and William married during the time that polygamists were being arrested, Agnes frequently had to go into hiding to avoid federal marshals. Her daughter Lula Roskelley Mortensen (born 1899) recalled hearing about that time period. When her mother was expecting her first son, she "was never seen by anyone nor was she ever out of the room until after dark." When Leonard was born prematurely on September 16, 1888, "he looked like a little shriveled up old man."

As Agnes had more children, she "had to teach them that they didn't know what their name was; they didn't know where they lived; they didn't know who their dad or mother was." Lula explained why: "The deputy marshals would corner the kids and get them to tell them who their dad and mother were and where they lived . . . in order to track down the polygamists."

Later William, Margaret, and Agnes no longer had to hide from the law, but that did not eliminate their problems. When William homesteaded land in Weston, Idaho, just over the Utah-Idaho boundary, he took Margaret, leaving Agnes in Smithfield. Margaret returned to Smithfield, and William built a large home for Margaret and a small home for Agnes. One of Margaret's children explained that it was because Margaret had more surviving children.

But the problems did not end with housing. As the first wife, Margaret was responsible for dividing all the goods between the families. All the food, for example, came first to Margaret. She divided it based on the number of children in her family and the number in Agnes'. Then rather than delivering the goods to Agnes, Margaret simply left them on Agnes' pantry window sill outside of the house. While Margaret's daughter Rebecca Roskelley Lewis said that her mother tried to be fair, Lula said that the pantry window was "a watchtower to observe the happenings in our home."

As a result, Margaret and Agnes rarely communicated, talking occasionally as they worked in the raspberry patch. They did not visit each other even when their other sisters came from out of town. Roxey Roskelley Rogers, Margaret's daughter said, "In my day Mother and Auntie were not close at all. . . . I just always felt like they didn't want to be close and forgive, no matter what. . . . I have sat at church more than once with Mother on one side and with Auntie on the other side of me. They didn't speak."

Children from both families described Margaret as a domineering woman who got what she wanted. Even her children thought she was hard to get along with. Rebecca Roskelley Lewis said Agnes had no "spunk" and was submissive. Lula asked her mother why she agreed to marry her sister's husband. "You must have known what a troublemaker she was as your older sister." Agnes simply replied, "Well, I guess we expected everyone to be about perfect, living in the principle." According to the children, William was easygoing and wanted peace, so he usually gave in to Margaret.

Agnes died in 1945, William followed in 1948, and Margaret died in 1952. Lula explained that her mother, Agnes, had declared that she had had enough of William Roskelley in this life and the hereafter.[2] The Roskelley experience was unhappy from Lula's point of view because all three of Kimball Young's factors—personality, financial arrangements, and husband's treatment—were negative. Even Margaret's children recognized the problems.

Edward McGregor Patterson

The Roskelley example, however, was not typical of the families I studied. In most cases, the husband and wives worked together and overlooked differences. Edward McGregor Patterson also married sisters, but his wives had a better experience. Edward was born in England in 1841. He moved to Utah, where he met Mary Thompson, a Danish immigrant who was born in 1853. They married in 1868. The family moved to Bloomington, Idaho, a small community on Bear Lake that crosses the Utah-Idaho border. In 1882 he married Mary's sister, Sarah, who was born in Bloomington six months after her older sister married.

Edward was called on a mission to avoid the marshals. While he was gone, the wives worked together on a loom and sold rag rugs to people in the Bear Lake Valley. Even when Edward was around, the wives worked together. They did their laundry together, and Sarah made clothes for the girls while Mary made clothes for the boys. Mary once commented, "We took up the trade of weaving. When I say we, I mean my sister Sarah and family. We are all one family."

Sarah had a baby, Venna, on July 14, 1906, and died one month later. Edward followed in 1909, but Mary lived until 1947. Mary took Sarah's children and raised them. Mary and her older half-sisters were the only mothers that Venna knew.[3]

Daily Life

How did Mormon families adapt to the unusual marriage practice of polygamy? What were the living arrangements? What were the visiting arrangements? How did the families interact? There was no one way. The following description of plural families applies to those in which there were two or three plural wives.

Role of Men, Women, and Children

The LDS Church is patriarchal; men have the authority. All worthy men hold a lay priesthood. While women play an important role in the Church and the family, they do not hold the priesthood. LDS men and women attend the temple and make the same covenants, but in the traditional pattern, men are (and were) the head of the household. Some critics insist that LDS women are forced (and were forced) to follow their husbands' leadership. Many LDS women disagree. They point out that they are equal partners with their husbands. Still, the priesthood authority belongs only to men, just as the ability to bear children belongs only to the women.

This pattern of men leading and women and children following was typical during the Victorian period when the Mormon Church practiced polygamy. Since the Industrial Revolution, men have become the breadwinners and worked outside the home. Women have worked in the home and cared for the children. Gradually children were no longer seen as little adults who were farmed out to be apprentices. Instead, childhood became a privileged time in which young people went to school and played.

The Victorian focus was on the arrangement between a husband and wife. So it is ironic that the Mormon plural families adapted this

Christopher Jones Arthur Family

Victorian ideal to fit polygamy. Kimball Young observed, "After all, the plural family was really but an appendage to the basic patriarchal monogamous family. In matters such as the location of the families—whether under the same roof all together or in separate households in the same community or in different localities—there were no definite rules."[4]

My research has shown that Young was right. There were no definite rules, but there were some common patterns for living arrangements, visiting schedules, and daily life.

Living Arrangements[5]

The ideal for Mormon plural families was to have separate homes for each wife. The belief was that every woman wanted to be the queen of her own castle. Separate homes were not always possible, however. After Edward Christian Eyring married his sister-in-law, the two wives shared a house until he completed a home for his second wife. Camilla Eyring Kimball, the oldest child of the first wife, Caroline, was so upset that her father had married another wife that she gave the new wife, Emma, the ugliest silverware when she set the table.

Edward was a successful businessman in Mexico, and his wives enjoyed the benefits of his income. The women occasionally worked together, but they had separate homes and all the comforts of life. The Mexican Revolution change that. When the Eyrings decided to leave Mexico, Edward bought a home in Pima, Arizona, and then added another so the homes were next to each other. Each wife had a separate home, but they had a shared area.

William Archibald Murray and his two wives, Amanda Bailey Murray and Sarah Jane Park Murray, split William's time based on their children's needs. One wife lived on the farm with the boys, who could help with the work. The other wife lived in town with the children who were going to school or working.

James Carson Allen and his wives, Betsy Allen and Ellen Allen, lived in Cove, Utah, a town on the Utah-Idaho border. When the children got old enough to attend the LDS Church-owned Brigham Young College in Logan, fifteen miles away, Betsy moved to Logan and Nellie stayed in Cove with the younger children. The families switched places for Thanksgiving and Christmas holidays.

Visiting Schedules[6]

My study of 156 families matched Kimball Young's fifty families for visiting schedules. The types of schedules broke into four equal categories: one-fourth of the husbands alternated daily, one-fourth changed on a weekly basis, one-fourth had an irregular schedule, and the final fourth had a two-day, three-day, or monthly schedule.

David Henry Cannon had three wives. According to his son Douglas he was at his mother's home "every third day, regular as clockwork." Douglas had a special assignment of taking a shaving kit to the home where his father would be staying.

Edward Christian Eyring kept a weekly schedule. He would pack his bags and move to the other wife's home every Saturday. Even when the homes were next door, he lived with the one wife for a week. This does not mean that he did not see the other family daily. According to son LeRoy, every night Edward would visit the other home at bedtime and kiss the children good night.

Edward William Payne of Mexico was separated from his first wife, but his other two wives, Lucy Alice Farr and Rosalia Tenney Farr, tried to make things as equal as possible. Edward went where he was needed. According to a son Eldon

Payne, his father's schedule "wasn't a hard and fast rule like some people."

If wives did not live in the same community, visits could not be as regular. When one wife lived in Canada and another lived in the United States, visits were especially rare. Heber Simeon Allen, who served as stake president in Raymond, Alberta, came to Salt Lake City to see his family there only twice a year for general conference, staying a month each time.

Impact of Polygamy

Women

Polygamy was hard on both men and women. It meant dividing affections usually reserved for one person. But the question most frequently asked is how the women felt about it. The answer is that women reacted in every way imaginable. Most plural wives accepted polygamy because it was God's commandment. However, their public statements did not always match their private journal comments.

Emmeline B. Wells, twice a plural wife, epitomized the dilemmas that Mormon women faced. Wells was the editor of the *Woman's Exponent*, a paper written by Mormon women but not an official Church publication; a wife of Church leader Daniel H. Wells; leader of a grain storage program, and later president of the Relief Society. A highly visible and involved woman, she spoke publicly about the virtues of plural marriage. As Carol Cornwall Madsen explained in her biography of Wells, "Many columns of the paper [the *Woman's Exponent*] were devoted to the defense of [polygamy]. Although the primary justification for plural marriage was obedience to God's will, Latter-day Saints debated the question on the moral and social grounds argued by their detractors."

Wells said "polygamy advanced woman's status by making her less subordinate and more independent than monogamy."

She also felt that it taught "patience, generosity, tolerance, and sororal [sisterly] affections." In addition, it eliminated a "double moral standard" that men did not have to be loyal to their spouses, but women did. And plural marriage gave women the chance to marry and have children. Madsen concluded, "In other words, [Wells] maintained, it promoted Christian virtues and the qualities of selfless womanhood" so common in the Victorian ideal.[7]

But Wells's journal showed a different side of polygamy. In her case, it was that of a woman left alone. Emmeline was the plural wife to two men. After it appeared that her first husband had deserted her, she married Newell K. Whitney in 1845. She loved being a part of the Whitney family and had two children with Newell. Two years after he died in 1850, she became the seventh wife of Daniel H. Wells, a good friend of Whitney. Emmeline had three daughters from this plural union. Wells was a counselor to Brigham Young, mayor of Salt Lake City, University of Deseret (now the University of Utah) chancellor, and, among many other public offices, was the city's public works superintendent. All of his wives except Emmeline lived together. She missed association with her husband.[8]

Emmeline could sometimes rationalize this separation. She wrote in 1875, "My husband is too much engrossed with public affairs to devote much time or even sympathy to his family. . . . Therefore the care and responsibility devolves upon the mother." But the year before she had lamented the separation. "Oh, if my husband could love me even a little and not seem so perfectly indifferent to any sensation of that kind. He cannot know the craving of my nature, he is surrounded with love on every side, and I am cast out. Oh my poor aching heart. Where shall it rest its burden, only on the Lord, only to Him can I look. Every other avenue seems closed against me. . . . . I have no one to go to for comfort or shelter, no strong arm to lean upon, no bosom bared for me, no protection or comfort in my husband."[9]

Martha Hughes Cannon's letters to her husband, Angus, from her hiding place in England in 1886–87 reflect a similar dilemma. Historians Constance L. Leiber and John Sillito summarized her feelings. Martha struggled to accept polygamy, but she wrote, "The knowledge that it is God's plan . . . is the only thing that saves [me and others] from despair—almost madness I fear." But as her time in England continued, Leiber and Sillito explained, "Mattie's letters changed in tone. They became full of pain, jealousy, loneliness, and depression, lacking the usual 'good-humor in spite of trials' of her earlier letters."[10]

Cannon, however, had options not available to all plural wives. After she returned from England, she had a medical practice and taught classes in nursing. In 1896 she ran for the Utah State Senate as a Democrat. One of the Republican candidates she beat was her husband.[11]

Because of women like Wells and Cannon, some scholars argue that polygamy was a liberating factor for Mormon women. Historian Joan Iverson has called plural wives "feminists." Examples include Romania Pratt and Ellis Reynolds Shipp, who went to medical school in Pennsylvania while their sister wives took care of their children. That is the exact opposite of the nineteenth century view that polygamy was "a slavery which debases and degrades womanhood, mother, [and] family."

But did polygamy have that impact on all Mormon women? I argue no. Rather than being "decades ahead of their sisters in the American East in economics and professional opportunities," as historian Maureen Ursenbach Beecher concluded, at first their work "varied little from women's work anywhere else in the western civilization."[12]

My research group shows that most plural wives, like their

monogamous counterparts, depended upon their husbands for support. Of the 225 wives for whom I could find information, only 9 percent received no support from their husbands, and only 3 percent received only minimal support. The remaining 88 percent divided the support of their families with their husbands.

Plural wives assisted their husbands in traditional ways. Of 291 polygamous wives, 20 percent worked outside the home at some time, but none of them did so continually. The remaining sold farm goods (22.4 percent), used home skills (23.4 percent), or used careful budgeting (32 percent).[13]

But life is not only economics. How did plural wives get along with their husbands' other spouses? With separate homes, they did not have to interact with each other if they did not want to. But some worked together. Whatever the relationships, religious commitment helped the women overlook jealousies. But there was no clear pattern on how to relate to other wives, as in other cultures. So the wives used their monogamous experiences as models. Plural wives were often called sister wives. As mentioned earlier, in about 25 percent of my study, the wives were actually sisters. When there was a major difference in age, there was even a mother-daughter quality to the relationship.

Of course, humans often have jealousies and want attention. Rosalia Tenney Payne, the plural wife of E. W. Payne, showed some of those tendencies. First she explained, "I married with an intense desire to make a go of it." But how did she get along with the second wife? "I'd get along if it cost me my skin. . . . I felt that I was living a holy principle and that I must conform my life to it. Polygamy makes people more tolerant, more understanding, and more unselfish. It gives them more contact with reality and a wider circle to love. . . . It's not an easy way to live. We never fully conquer ourselves. And always it is the little things that make it hard, the little foxes always upset the vine, you know. It's not jealousy so much for I had my mind made up to that, but the constant pressure of adjusting yourself to another woman."[14]

But coping with jealousy varied with each wife. Their reactions were personality based and varied. Some women served their husbands' other wives and learned to love them. Samuel Roskelley had six wives, and their relationships show the wide variety of experience. Mary Jane Rigby Roskelley, his fourth wife, lived with Mary Roberts, his second wife, in a one-room log house. Mary Jane explained, "We had our first babies there and did all our work together." By working "shoulder to shoulder," the two wives "got along famously." When Samuel was with his other wives, Mary Jane admitted she was jealous but reassured herself, "I believe he loved me as much as any woman he ever had. I have letters to prove that."

But not all of Samuel's wives were as compatible. Emma Hansen, a daughter of the fifth wife, Margaret Rigby Roskelley, explained that although her mother and Mary Jane were sisters, she was closer to Mary, the third wife. "Aunt [Mary] Jane was high strung. She just seemed a little harder to get along with than the others."

When Samuel married his sixth wife, Sarah Maud Burton, Mary Jane said that the wives had a common enemy. No one liked her. Sarah was much younger, and Mary Jane questioned her husband's motives for marrying her. Mary Jane said, "I used to hear that when you can't get along with anybody, you should just leave them alone. That is what we did with Maud. We didn't treat Maud ugly, but we just let her alone." It was hard because Samuel "spent more time with her than with us." She could make him "believe the moon was made of green cheese. She's caused me more trouble than a little bit." Even when Maude tried to visit the other wives, she was not welcomed.[15]

Louis Brandley, the son of John Theodore Brandley and second wife Margaret (Maggie) Brandley, grew up in Richfield, Utah. According to Louis, his father met his first wife, Marie Elizabeth Naegeli Brandley, while on a mission in Switzerland. Theodore returned to Utah, and Marie and her mother followed. Theodore and Marie married in 1872 when John was twenty-one and Marie was eighteen. Marie was Theodore's "first love," and their relationship was "true and sweet."

Ten years later, Theodore married eighteen-year-old Margaret Keeler Brandley. Louis saw the marriage as following Church leaders, but it was not based on love. It was a "business arrangement." Margaret simply recorded in her journal, "Today I married Theodore Brandley." She expressed no romantic love. She was following Church leaders' advice, and Theodore was worthy of having another wife.

When Theodore went on another mission to Switzerland in 1876, he met Rosina Elizabeth (Eliza) Zaugg and Emma Biefer. The mission president asked Theodore to take Eliza and a friend on a picnic. Eliza told Louis that was when the romance began.

When Theodore returned home, his first wife, Marie, built a new home and bakery in Richfield. After Marie died in 1892, Theodore asked Maggie to care for the house and Marie's eight children. But Maggie had poor health and could not care for the business and the extra children. So Theodore hired housekeepers, including Eliza and Emma. He married them after the Manifesto. Some records say in 1891 and 1893; others say in 1901 and 1903. Eliza had her first child in 1902.

Theodore was among a second group of Latter-day Saints who moved to Canada for economic reasons, taking his wife Eliza with him. Emma moved to Salt Lake City. Maggie lived in Richfield. These two wives saw Theodore only when he came to Utah twice a year for general conference. According to Louis, Marie and Eliza were the preferred wives. The other two were "Isaiah's class of women." Isaiah 4:1 reads, "In that day seven women shall take hold of one man, saying, We will eat our own bread and wear our own apparel; only let us be called by thy name, to take away our reproach."

Because Emma and Maggie were in the same position, Louis said, they were "the closest of friends. They shared the same faith, the same trust, the same hopes and the same husband. Significantly, they [also] shared the same frustrations, the same poverty, the same loneliness, the same widowhood."[16]

Men

While the focus is usually on women, men also had unique arrangements. Because they were expected to support their families, they had to split their resources. For those who were farmers, having additional family members meant that everyone helped with the work. Those who were professionals had a higher salary. So, as might be expected, most of the polygamous husbands in my study were owners of farms, ranches, or another business (57.8 percent) or professionals (20.6 percent). Other professions were skilled craftsmen, white collar, and semiskilled or unskilled laborers.

But economics did not always remain the same for men. In Mexico, Charles Edmund Richardson did well. In Colonia Diaz, he taught school and ran a blacksmith shop and a gristmill. He answered stake president Anthony W. Ivins's call to study law in Mexico City. He took one of his three wives to the capital city for four years and graduated with honors. His businesses supported the other wives while he was away. Later he traveled among the colonies and moved a wife to Colonia Juarez, near the local government seat of Nuevo Casa Grande. There he married a fourth wife. Hazel Richardson Taylor, a daughter of his first wife, recalled that her father "was as well-to-do as the average man was, but when he divided it into four families, he had to watch his pennies. . . . We dressed well; we ate well; we had comfortable homes. But I wouldn't say that we were well-to-do. We never could afford to live lavishly."

When the Richardsons left Mexico during the Mexican Revolution in 1912, however, their lives changed. Edmund could not practice law, but he returned to Mexico to help settle the Mormons' land claims against the Mexicans. He purchased several farms and lost them. For example, his two farms near Duncan, Arizona, were flooded when the railroad drains over-flowed; he lost another farm in a lawsuit. His wives attempted to file on homesteads. Edmunds tried teaching again. He got a teaching certificate and taught Spanish-speaking students for three years, away from his family. But his salary as an elementary school teacher was not enough to support four families, so he tried unsuccessfully to mine. His gristmill failed when the established mills took him to court for adding competition.[17]

Children

During the Victorian period, children were the responsibility of their mothers. It did not matter whether the families were polygamous or monogamous. Fathers were frequently absent. Even if they did not have to go to another house, they had to go to work in town or on the farm. Mothers felt a special bond to their children. That relationship may have been stronger when the woman shared a husband, but it was always stronger than between a child and a father. However, when polygamous families were compared with monogamous ones, the children from monogamous families were closer to their fathers.

As with all aspects of plural marriage, there are no typical relationships between children and their parents. A few examples show the variety. Annie Clark Tanner, whose autobiography of growing up in a polygamous household and then being a plural wife is frequently quoted, said, "As I have observed monogamy, the husband and wife rearing a family have a common interest. They are a team working together for the advantages of the children. In polygamy the man's interests are scattered." Tanner's statement reflects her experience in polygamy. Her husband wanted her to move to Canada; Annie refused because she wanted a good education for her children.

Archie L. Jenkins had a telling story about his relationship with his mother and father. After describing how close he was to his father, he said, "My father never showed any sentimental feelings toward our family to speak of, which we felt like we were missing as we grew up. . . . We respected Father but he never gave us a chance to really love him as nonpolygamous families seemed to enjoy with a father patriarch dedicated to one family."

But polygamy gave children "other mothers" as well. Few children in my sample discussed their relationships with their father's other wives. When asked to described them in oral history interviews, they talked about the physical characteristics of the other women, along with their positive and sometimes negative characteristics. There were exceptions. Joseph W. Pratt's mother taught school, and his father's other wife, Dora, "was just like a mother to me, especially being Mother's own sister. . . . Aunt Dora kept the house and took care of us. . . . I thought at the time that was just the way things ought to be . . . but after I got older I decided Aunt Dora was something special."

Most of the time children referred to their fathers' other wives as "aunt," whether they were actually sisters of their mothers. The term was a way to show respect and still display affection. In rare cases, the first wife was much older. Esther Webb Pope called her father's first wife "Sister Webb." When the wife was younger, sometimes even close to the age of the older children, the children used the wife's first name. Catherine Scott Brown said, "We always called [father's other wife] Zilly; she was just like one of the girls."

Some children referred to the other wife as a second mother, of whom they could ask anything. Others were afraid to ask the other wife for something. The children of Henry Christian Eyring were honest in their feelings about the other wife, who was their mother's sister. LeRoy Eyring, a son of the second wife, Emma, said that Caroline, the first wife, was "certainly not a grandmother. We called her Auntie. That was the proper address for her. I suppose we thought of her more like an aunt, but certainly a very stern aunt and one that I, at least, was afraid of." Caroline, her mother's namesake, said that her relationship with Emma "was not comparable in any way to my relationship with my mother. I liked her and thought a lot of her, . . . and I thought often if she had been just an aunt removed, we would have been very close to her or maybe closer."

Polygamy also gave children additional brothers and sisters. Again, the relationships varied from very close to no relationship. Two examples show the extremes. Frank Romney's response was typical: "I had a friend call me one day, and she said, 'Are Gaskell and George Romney your half brothers?' I said, 'No, I don't have any half brothers. They all have two eyes and two ears and two arms and two legs." He continued: "My childhood life was especially happy because of the many brothers and sisters that I had. I had eight full brothers and sisters and sixteen half brothers and sisters. My half brothers and sisters sometimes treated me better than my immediate family."

But that was not always the case. George S. Tanner said of his half brother Clifford, who was only four months older: "We should have been the closest of friends. We should have enjoyed each other thoroughly." Instead, "this brother of mine, Clifford, and I battled."

Clifford started school before George, but George skipped grades. "Before he graduated from the eighth grade," George explained, "I was two years ahead." George added that part of the reason for the animosity was that "there was jealousy between my mother and his mother and there was jealousy between me and him."[18]

Louis Brandley did not know the children of his father's third wife, Eliza, because her family lived in Canada. However, he responded to his father's request to move to Canada to help on the farm. When his mother passed away, he continued to live in Canada and got to know Eliza's children. Louis felt that Eliza gave "a full measure of family care as though we had been her own flesh and blood. . . . As soon as we got there she took us into her home and into her heart. . . . There was no difference between my mother's children and Aunt Marie's [the first wife] children in her mind." He added, "She was devoted to her own children and she guarded them like a mother hen. That was understandable."[19]

Notes

1. Kimball Young, *Isn't One Wife Enough?* (New York: Henry Holt & Co., 1954), 447.
2. Jessie L. Embry, *Mormon Polygamous Families: Life in the Principle* (Salt Lake City: University of Utah Press, 1987), 21–22, 83, 124, 129, 142, 146.
3. Ibid., 98, 102, 141.
4. Young, *Isn't One Wife Enough,* 153–54.
5. Embry, *Mormon Polygamous Families,* 75–80.
6. Ibid., 80-83
7. Carol Cornwall Madsen, *An Advocate for Women: The Public Life of Emmeline B. Wells, 1870–1920* (Provo, Utah: Brigham Young University, 2006), 48–49.

8.   Ibid., 19–20.

9.   Ibid, 7; Carol Cornwall Madsen, "Emmeline B. Wells, 'Am I Not a Woman and a Sister?'" *Brigham Young University Studies* 22 (Spring 1982): 167.

10.   Constance L. Lieber and John Sillito, *Letters from Exile: The Correspondence of Martha Hughes Cannon and Angus M. Cannon, 1886–1888* (Salt Lake City: Signature Books, 1989), xxi–xxii.

11.   Ibid., xxiv.

12.   Maureen Ursenbach Beecher, "Under the Sunbonnets: Mormon Women with Faces," *BYU Studies* 16 (Summer 1981): 471–84; Maureen Ursenbach Beecher, "Women's Work on the Frontier, *Utah Historical Quarterly* 49 (Summer 1981): 279–90.

13.   Embry, *Mormon Polygamous Families*, 94–97.

14.   Ibid., 137–41.

15.   Ibid., 146.

16.   Ibid., 56–67, 95, 140.

17.   Ibid., 90–94.

18.   Ibid., 151–73.

19.   Ibid., 165.

Summary

The Mormon practice of polygamy in the nineteenth century is not well understood. This book has tried to answer some of the common questions about this famous practice among members of The Church of Jesus Christ of Latter-day Saints.

Almost everywhere Latter-day Saints go, they get asked about polygamy. When Utah governor George D. Clyde and his wife went to Latin America in the 1950s, a guest at a reception asked how many wives he had. The governor replied, "I just brought the one with me." When African-American Larry Troutman joined the Church in 1984, his mother asked, "What? The one where they have all the different wives?" When I served an LDS mission in Halifax, Nova Scotia, Canada, a man figured out a clever way to get rid of my companion and me. Immediately after we introduced ourselves, he said, "Isn't that the church where you can have more than one wife? Would both of you be available?" We left with no further comment.[1]

I believe that the major question most non-Latter-day Saints have is why members of the Church agreed to go

Wives of Joseph W. Summerhays

against their traditional beliefs and marry in polygamy. Some Latter-day Saints would ask the same question. Polygamy does not seem to fit the pattern of a church that now upholds the traditional family of father, mother, and children as the ideal, a church that has issued "The Family: A Proclamation to the World," which focuses on the roles of father as breadwinner and mother as homemaker.

There is really only one way to answer those questions. Church leaders and members perceived plural, or celestial, marriage as a commandment of God. Even believing that, most Mormons did not practice polygamy. Church leaders accepted polygamy and endured the legislation passed again them because they felt that they were doing the will of God. They may have believed, as Christ taught, that "blessed are they which are persecuted for righteousness' sake" (Matthew 5:10).

To understand polygamy, we must accept that God speaks to man and that His commandments are important. However, it is always difficult to know whether such promptings are from God or from a person's own desires. I have to answer that question for myself. I cannot answer it for others, especially not for those who have passed away. My best answer for why members of The Church of Jesus Christ of Latter-day Saints accepted polygamy is to quote their reasons.

Mary Jane Done Jones, the first wife of Timothy Jones, said, "Polygamy was a great trial to any woman. And it was just as hard on the man. He had to learn to adjust to his women and his troubles were made worse by the women having to learn to adjust too." She continued: "Polygamy was a great principle and we were taught to believe in it. I know that it does bring added blessings if one lives it the best she knows how. It makes one more unselfish and more willing to see and understand other people. After you learn to give in and consider other people, it makes you feel less selfish in all your relations."

Edward Christian Eyring wrote in his autobiography: "This record shows that at least part of the families making up this account have lived in Mormon polygamy. This will no doubt be obnoxious to some who may read it. Even some of our descendants may wish it had been otherwise. I wish to impress this fact upon the minds of my children that to discredit the principle of plural marriage is the same as discrediting any principle of the Mormon Doctrine. . . . I testify to you that I know my father entered into the principle in full faith of receiving a generous reward from our Heavenly Father for this honest effort to live it properly. The same can be said of my father-in-law, Miles P. Romney, and I testify to you myself after twenty-eight years of experience in trying to live it that I know the principle is divine."

Children expressed similar feelings. Ivan R. Richardson explained, "If I was to judge polygamy solely on the basis of what happened in our family, I would have to say I'm in favor of it. It made us better people. It taught me to be unselfish. It taught us to work for a common goal with others."

Even those who experienced hardships could not discount it because it was their life. Louis Brandley, whose mother raised her children alone while his father was in Canada, said, "From my childhood I have accepted polygamy as the Lord's way for my mother and her family. My first feeling is that it brought misery to the people who tried to live it mainly because they weren't prepared. My next feeling is that I can't discount polygamy because it was responsible for my birth."[2]

I will never fully understand Mormon polygamy in this life. It is one of my questions—although not on the top of my list—for a loving God if I am fortunate to see Him in the next life. I cannot imagine living polygamy. But I admire the people who attempted to live what they felt was a commandment of God.

Selected Readings

It is difficult to recommend a few of the many books available on polygamy. Each book has added something new to the understanding of the practice. The best overview of writings about polygamy until 1987 was Richard Van Wagoner's *Mormon Polygamy*. Van Wagoner summarizes many studies. While his book does not have new interpretations, it does put many thoughts about polygamy in one place. My book *Mormon Polygamous Families: Life in the Principle* uses oral histories to explain how families were organized. It asks questions similar to the ones that Kimball Young asked in *Isn't One Wife Enough?*

More recent studies include Sarah Barringer Gordon's *The Mormon Question: Polygamy and Constitutional Conflict in Nineteenth Century America*, Kathryn M. Daynes's *More Wives than One: Transformation of the Mormon Marriage System, 1840–1910,* and B. Carmon Hardy's *Solemn Covenant: The Mormon Polygamous Passage.*

Note

1. Jessie L. Embry, *Mormon Polygamous Families: Life in the Principle* (Salt Lake City: University of Utah Press, 1987), xiii.
2. Ibid, 187–92.

Author Biographical Information

Jessie L. Embry is the Associate Director of the Charles Redd Center for Western Studies and an Associate Research Professor at Brigham Young University. She was a member of the first oral history class offered by the Redd Center in 1973. She has been in charge of the oral history programs at the Redd Center since 1979. She is the author of seven other books and over one hundred articles. Her books include Mormon Polygamous Families: Life in the Principle (Salt Lake City: University of Utah Press, 1987) and three books on ethnic Mormons. Her research focuses on Utah, Western American, Mormon, and women's history and nearly all of her publications use oral histories.

SETTING THE RECORD STRAIGHT SERIES

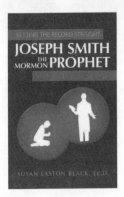

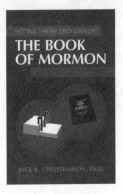

To learn more about these and other Millennial Press
titles, visit www.millennialpress.com. To purchase
these books visit wherever books are sold.